Complete Guide to
Sport Education

Daryl Siedentop, PED

The Ohio State University

Peter A. Hastie, PhD

Auburn University

Hans van der Mars, PhD

Oregon State University

Human Kinetics

Library of Congress Cataloging-in-Publication Data

Siedentop, Daryl.
 Complete guide to sport education / Daryl Siedentop, Peter A. Hastie, Hans van der Mars.
  p. cm.
 Rev. ed. of: Sport education / Daryl Siedentop, editor. c1994.
 Includes bibliographical references and index.
 ISBN 0-7360-4380-2 (soft cover)
 1. Sports for children--Study and teaching. I. Hastie, Peter A., 1959- II. Van der Mars, Hans, 1955- III.
Sport education. IV. Title.
 GV709.2.S663 2004
 796.07'1--dc22

                              2004004526

ISBN-10: 0-7360-4380-2
ISBN-13: 978-0-7360-4380-9

Acquisitions Editor: Scott Wikgren; **Developmental Editor:** Melissa Feld; **Assistant Editor:** Maggie Schwarzentraub and Kathleen Bernard; **Copyeditor:** Joanna Hatzopolous Portman; **Proofreader:** Sarah Wiseman; **Indexer:** Betty Frizzéll; **Permission Manager:** Dalene Reeder; **Graphic Designer:** Fred Starbird; **Graphic Artist:** Denise Lowry; **Cover Designer:** Jack W. Davis; **Illustrator:** Kelly Hendren; **Printer:** United Graphics

Printed in the United States of America   10   9   8   7

The paper in this book is certified under a sustainable forestry program.

Human Kinetics
Web site: www.HumanKinetics.com

United States: Human Kinetics
P.O. Box 5076
Champaign, IL 61825-5076
800-747-4457
e-mail: humank@hkusa.com

Canada: Human Kinetics
475 Devonshire Road, Unit 100
Windsor, ON N8Y 2L5
800-465-7301 (in Canada only)
e-mail: info@hkcanada.com

Europe: Human Kinetics
107 Bradford Road
Stanningley
Leeds LS28 6AT, United Kingdom
+44 (0)113 255 5665
e-mail: hk@hkeurope.com

Australia: Human Kinetics
57A Price Avenue
Lower Mitcham, South Australia 5062
08 8372 0999
e-mail: info@hkaustralia.com

New Zealand: Human Kinetics
Division of Sports Distributors NZ Ltd.
P.O. Box 300 226 Albany
North Shore City, Auckland
0064 9 448 1207
e-mail: info@humankinetics.co.nz

Contents

Preface

Complete Guide to Sport Education is designed for physical education teachers and students preparing to become physical education teachers. The book provides a clear and comprehensive explanation of the Sport Education curriculum and instruction model and includes all the information needed to use the model. The book will also be very helpful to teachers who have already adopted the model because it is more comprehensive than the initial book on Sport Education (Siedentop, 1994); it includes more supporting materials for doing Sport Education, and we have all learned so much more about how to apply the model to different activities.

Sport Education is now recognized throughout the world as a viable model for physical education from third through twelfth grade. Examples of successful implementation of the model with activities as varied as weightlifting and popular dance, as well as many sports, have appeared in professional journals throughout the world. An increasing awareness of the Sport Education model exists among teachers, and it is increasingly being taught to prospective physical education teachers as a viable approach to providing a quality physical education experience to students. This increased interest in Sport Education has created the need for this comprehensive and useful text.

Complete Guide to Sport Education provides a thorough explanation of the goals and purpose of the model, carefully describes its curricular and instructional implications, and then describes in great detail how to implement it. You will learn how to select activities, how to organize teams, how to decide which student roles to use, how to modify activities, how to design competition formats, and, finally, how to use all this information to design sport education seasons. The text also includes a detailed plan for building class management routines that are necessary for the Sport Education model to be implemented successfully and a comprehensive behavior development system based on the concept of fair play. A thorough chapter on assessment is provided, as well as chapters devoted to creating a festive environment for Sport Education, integrating other subjects into the model, and extending participation outside of class time.

The book is organized in a manner that lets you understand the model, then provides step-by-step information that allows you to make decisions about how you want to implement the model in your local situation. The text includes a CD-ROM in which you will find all the information and forms necessary to plan and implement Sport Education seasons. Icons appear at various points within the text to alert you to resources available in the CD-ROM. These resources are quite varied, including items such as captain contracts, fair play posters, seasonal planning sheets, competition format sheets, awards, and the like.

The book includes evidence from national trials of the model in New Zealand and Australia, as well as evidence from numerous research studies that have assessed the viability and power of the model to achieve important goals in physical education. Throughout the book we include quotations from teachers and students who have experienced the model, testifying to the positive effects it has for students of all ability levels. The evidence allows us to be confident that students at all levels have valued their Sport Education experiences and tend to see the model as an improvement over more traditional approaches to physical education.

The content and style of the book are meant to be of practical value to those who want to implement the model. All of the steps and procedures suggested have been used by teachers. We owe an enormous debt to the creative physical educators who have extended the model to show that it can be applied to various activities, some of which are not typically considered to be sports.

Introduction

This practical book was written for teachers, whom we know lead busy lives. They have little enough time for planning for the next class or day or unit, let alone for quiet reflection on the larger issues inherent in the subject matter they teach. We hope this book will encourage teachers and prospective teachers to adopt the Sport Education model. We expect that the detailed information in the book and the resources in the accompanying CD-ROM will help them use the model well without having to spend endless hours looking for or creating materials and plans. We also hope that learning about and using the Sport Education model will help physical educators to think about and understand the important potential that good sport has both in the lives of individuals and in the health and well-being of the culture.

All who read this book will understand the dark side of sport. We know the terrible stories about adults becoming violent because they disliked something in a youth sport game in which their children participated. We are aware that many youngsters get turned off to sport because of the ceaseless pressure they feel from the adults around them. We are troubled that excesses and inappropriate practices in high school, college, and professional sport are all too commonplace. A major purpose of Sport Education is for students to learn to distinguish between good sport and bad sport.

"Sports teach," said Wilfred Sheed (1995, p.16), "it is their nature. They teach fairness or cheating, teamwork or selfishness, compassion or coldness." In the opening chapter to this book you will learn that Sport Education has lofty goals. One goal is for girls and boys to learn fairness, teamwork, and compassion as they participate in sport. Another goal is for them to become more aware of what qualities and characteristics make sport good and to become motivated to work in their local communities to ensure that more people can experience good sport.

Part of the sport experience is being in the moment and relishing the feelings one gets from performing well, individually or as part of a team. Writing in the summer of 1992 as millions of people around the world watched the U.S. basketball Dream Team win the Olympic gold medal, the noted author Anna Quindlen described the magic of such moments.

> Catholic schoolgirls once played intramural basketball all winter long, and though it was with a smaller ball and slacker rules than the boys used—and though I traveled more often than I ever scored—it gave me a visceral feeling for the nonpareil grace, skill and teamwork of the sport. Not to mention that glow in your chest when the ball leaves your hands, arcs through the air with all eyes following, and falls almost inevitably through the hoop. Yessss . . . There's a moment when the ball arcs perfectly downward to the waiting web of the net—or when the words lie down just right on the page—that makes you feel as if you could live forever. (Quindlen, 1992, p. 3H)

Of course, we don't live forever, so experiences that give us that feeling should be cherished and protected. The sport education model has shown that it can provide such meaningful experiences for girls and boys, more and less skilled, abled and disabled.

So, despite the practical nature of this book, important personal and social goals need to be achieved. We describe these goals in the first chapter as the development of competent, enthusiastic, and literate sportspersons. We hope that as you work from day to day doing the often repetitive chores that effective teachers do, you keep sight of the larger goals and you take pleasure from watching your students operate within the Sport Education model, gaining both pleasure and a deeper meaning from their sport experience.

How to Use the CD-ROM

The Teacher Resources CD-ROM, included with the *Complete Guide to Sport Education,* offers numerous supporting materials for those who do Sport Education. We have made every effort to align the CD-ROM resources with the text. As you will see, the file folders on the CD-ROM are organized around the 11 chapters, with a few additional sets of resources. Thus, each chapter has its own resource folder. To get started, put the CD-ROM in your computer's CD drive and use your operating system to navigate the CD-ROM.

The icons that are located in the margins of the text are linked to the boldfaced words in the text and refer to the corresponding resource folder on the CD-ROM. Each icon has a number and a folder name. The number in the icon refers to the corresponding resource folder located on the CD-ROM. The icon's folder name refers to the folder within that specific resource folder where supporting resources can be found. In many cases additional subfolders are within each chapter's resource folder. Users can refer to the CD-ROM, which has a complete contents file, for a more detailed listing of all available resources.

Our overriding goal in the development of these resources is to offer teachers and students support in making Sport Education a successful experience for all. The resources were developed with readily available software programs within Microsoft Office®. We also recognize that teachers and students live in various contexts, so the materials may need to be adapted to fit "local conditions." Therefore, we encourage teachers to adapt the materials where they think it is needed or appropriate. We do ask that teachers continue to recognize the original source.

The resources and materials included are primarily for use by teachers and their students. They include posters, score sheets, competition format templates, sample contracts, Fair Play materials, and assessment templates. Several of the basic resources that would likely be used by students have been translated into Spanish. They are identified with "SPA" at the end of the file name.

For those teachers and students who have infused the use of notebook computers or personal digital assistants (PDAs) into their daily physical education experiences, several of the files that relate to such tasks as keeping score and assessment have several templates (developed in Microsoft Excel®) that are available in both regular print versions and electronic versions. With some practice, the management of information will get easier.

For those who teach curriculum and instruction courses in physical education teacher education programs, resource 14 includes supplementary materials such as discussion questions and chapter slides. Each chapter has a set of slides that highlight the main points of the chapter and include examples where appropriate.

We are always interested in receiving feedback from teachers who use Sport Education. We encourage users to send feedback and new ideas about the materials provided in the text and the CD-ROM. Send your comments to the following e-mail addresses:

Daryl Siedentop:	darylsiedentop@yahoo.com
Peter Hastie:	hastipe@mail.auburn.edu
Hans van der Mars:	hans.vandermars@oregonstate.edu

The Sport Education Model

14
Chapter Slides

Can you imagine a physical education program in which students significantly improve their abilities to perform activities skillfully and show increasing mastery of tactics? Can you imagine that in the same physical education program students are excited about what they are doing and share in the responsibilities of conducting class activities so that classes run smoothly with few disruptions? Is it also possible that in this very class students learn to appreciate and support the contributions of classmates of varying talents? And, to complete this picture, can you see that in this same program students with lower skill levels and students who typically do not participate are actively engaged and improving? Too good to be true? Not so! All of these outcomes, which are so difficult to see in many physical education programs, have been reported in evaluations of programs using the Sport Education model.

Sport Education (SE) is not a pie-in-the-sky idea that won't work in typical school settings. The model was slowly developed over several years by Daryl Siedentop working with physical educators in several schools in central Ohio. It has undergone national school-based trials in New Zealand and Australia. Sport Education has been used at all levels from the third grade in elementary schools through the twelfth grade in high schools. As you will see, the model is not only appropriate for team and individual sport activities, but also for dance and exercise activities. Sport Education has undergone several large-scale assessments as well as having been the focus of several research studies. We will share the results throughout the book, starting with results of a national evaluation of Sport Education in Australia, shown in figure 1.1.

Our purpose in writing this book is to help you to learn to do Sport Education. You may want to start with a basic version of Sport Education and expand it as you and your students gain more experience in the various features of the model. Then again, you may be more adventurous and jump right into the full model. Either way, the book will take you through all the decisions you have to make to get started and to develop the model in your physical education program. We will also show you the many different approaches that teachers have used to implement various aspects of the model. This book comes with a CD-ROM in which you will find all of the forms, posters, awards, contracts, scheduling formats, point systems, and the like that you will need to do Sport Education well. But first, we want you to understand what Sport Education is about, what it aims to achieve, and how it differs not only from conventional approaches to physical education programming but also from how girls and boys typically learn and experience sport in community and school sport programs. We suggest that before using the CD-ROM you review the section titled How to Use the CD-ROM (see p. xi) and also review "Navigating the CD-ROM," which can be found at the start of the CD-ROM.

Sport Education (SE) II Project Findings

- Some schools found that both absenteeism and nonparticipation rates fell under SE.
- Teachers observed that students spent more time talking about their PE experience both inside and outside of class.
- Students unanimously favored the SE approach over the PE approach.
- Students with lower ability levels were favored by the model, and they significantly improved their skills as a result of increased participation.
- It appears that SE is more gender inclusive than more traditional forms of PE.
- Our evaluation found that students expressed and displayed improved attitudes to sports as a result of their experiences in SE.
- In many cases students, who were previously habitual non-participants, became actively involved.
- Teachers claimed that students improved skills in areas other than techniques that were traditionally claimed but rarely achieved in PE.
- Participation levels were up; skills levels were up; and students were learning to umpire, manage, and coach more effectively.

Figure 1.1 Summary of results from the Sport Education (SE) II project, Sport and Physical Activity Research Centre in Perth, Australia.

Sport Education can be used for most physical activities in physical education programs. Sport Education is not just about mainstream sports such as basketball, softball, and touch football. The model has been used for weightlifting, dance forms, orienteering, and activities such as Frisbee or bocce (a game, similar to lawn bowling, that is popular in the Mediterranean countries of Europe). Why, then, do we call it Sport Education? First, Daryl Siedentop developed the model in the early 1980s as a result of his frustration with how sport activities were being taught in physical education. Typically, a short unit dominated by isolated skill drills was followed by poorly played games. Less-skilled students were often overshadowed by more-skilled students who dominated play, and many students were left frustrated or just plain bored. Sport Education was created to help all students be successful, enthused, and committed to doing better for themselves and their team. Thus, an initial purpose in naming the model was to emphasize its education benefits for all students.

Second, throughout most of the world, the term *sport* encompasses a much broader range of physical activities than in the United States, where it typically refers to competitive team and individual sports. For example, on U.S. sport talk shows, it is not uncommon to hear arguments that golf is not really a sport because competitors do not run and jump. This definition of sport is much too narrow. Sports are playful competitions whose outcomes are determined by physical skill, strategy, and chance (Loy & Kenyon, 1969; Siedentop, 2004). Most people would say that aerobic dance is not a sport. However, competitions are common in aerobic dance and people who have seen that activity in person immediately recognize the skill, strategy, and fitness of the performers. While aerobic dance may not be a sport, it can be done as a team activity with the creation of routines and judged in terms of set criteria for performance. So, aerobic dance is easily done in the Sport Education format.

MAJOR FEATURES OF THE SPORT EDUCATION MODEL

The idea for Sport Education grew over a five-year period when Daryl Siedentop and his doctoral students conducted numerous research studies aimed at understanding effective teaching in physical education. Each study required long-term observation of physical education classes. Many of the classes and teachers observed were effective by most standards. Classes were well organized. Students stayed on task. Few disruptions occurred. But what was absent was any sense of real excitement among the students. Most programs used the multiactivity curriculum approach with short activity units. The largest portion of class time was spent learning and practicing skills in drills that were not easily transferable to competitive play. Toward the end of the short unit, teams were organized to play games, but the team membership changed with each game. While observations of early unit skill practice showed that some students had begun to be able to do the skill drills fairly well, they could not transfer their skills to the complexity of a game context. As a result, the games were almost always poorly played. More-skilled students dominated the action. Less-skilled students found ways to stay out of the action, and they did not perform well when the action came their way. One would seldom reasonably conclude that students had authentic sport experiences. Games were so poorly played that one would likely conclude that these experiences would discourage students from wanting to learn or play those games outside of physical education class. This conclusion is especially true for invasion games such as basketball, all the football codes, and all the hockey codes where the pace of play is fast and the direction of action can change rapidly. Many students would become so bewildered and feel so out of place that they would do everything in their power to avoid being put in such an embarrassing situation.

These observations were in stark contrast to those of student participation in interscholastic sport, where enthusiasm and excitement often existed. Mastery of team tactics was just as or more important than isolated skill development. Indeed, the focus of many practice sessions was in preparation for a contest. The seasonal schedule gave both the meaning and the rhythm to the entire experience. The idea of being on a team was obviously important, giving the entire experience a special meaning. The experience was authentic. This does not suggest that student experience in interscholastic sport is perfect. It is not. Students typically do not get equal opportunity to practice and compete. Fair play is sometimes a casualty of an overemphasis on winning, and the result is often that students learn little about the sport other than specific techniques and tactics for the position they play and they have few responsibilities other than following the orders of the coaches.

> *This way is a lot more effective. Because then (in a traditional approach), he taught sport and you were rated on how you kicked or hit the ball. There were no real games. You just learned basic skills. Here you practice and play and referee. It is all run by kids and supervised by Mr. B but the students are doing it all. We are talking a lot more. We used to just run around like chickens without heads on. We definitely are learning more.*
>
> —Brett, eighth grade student, Australia

Nonetheless, it was out of this set of contrasting observations that the idea for Sport Education grew. The purpose was to develop a model for physical education that created an authentic sport experience for girls and boys, that was developmentally appropriate, and in which all participated equally. (See Siedentop [2002] for a history of the development of Sport Education.)

Figure 1.2 illustrates the primary features that typically characterize institutional forms of sport participation. These features give sport its special meaning and set it apart from other forms of physical activity. Sport is done in seasons. Players have affiliation with a team or club throughout a season. A schedule of formal competition defines the season and gives order to the organization of practice and competition sessions. It is the nature of sport for a season to culminate with an event that determines the seasonal champion. Records of all kinds are kept to judge success within a season and to provide a history and sense of standards for participating in that particular level of sport. The sport is festive, especially as a season moves toward its culmination. The festivity adds meaning to the participation and creates a context for exciting participation. None of these features is typically present in how sport is taught within physical education.

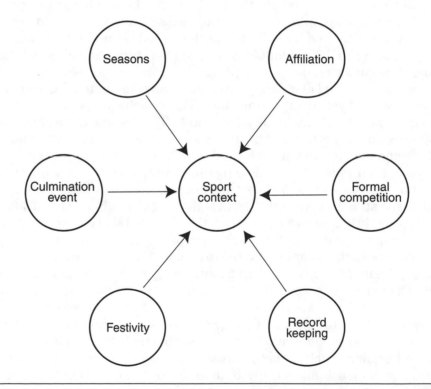

Figure 1.2   Primary features that define institutional sport and provide unique meanings for participation.

Seasons

Sport is done in seasons. Seasons are long enough to allow for a significant experience. A Sport Education season encompasses both practice and competition, leading to an event that brings the season to a close. This feature of Sport Education cannot be compromised. The exact length of a Sport Education season is determined partially by the frequency and duration of physical education classes. Sport Education seasons have been done successfully in as few as 12 elementary school class sessions of 45 minutes each and as long as half-semester seasons at the high school level. If a norm exists in the published literature on Sport Education, it seems to be 20 to 22 class sessions, but that may be because in a national trial of Sport Education in New Zealand, 20 class sessions was the minimum allowed for schools that participated in the trial. The scope and content of a high school team handball season is shown in figure 1.3.

Texas High School Team Handball Season

- The class has 34 students with the season lasting 21 class sessions.
- Students are divided into four coed teams.
- Teams represent four nations (Korea, Sweden, Norway, Russia).
- Team roles include coach, manager, fitness trainer, referee, scorer, and statistician.
- Techniques, tactics, and practice games are covered in the first part of the season.
- An Olympic tournament forms the primary competition schedule, double round-robin.
- Teams compete for gold, silver, and bronze medals.
- Closing ceremonies include a parade of athletes, display of national flags, and singing of anthems.
- An electronic scoreboard is used for all games.
- Students run the scoreboard and keep games statistics; statistics are printed as spreadsheets with pictures of the teams on a bulletin board.
- Use victory stands for medal ceremonies after the gold and bronze medal games.

Figure 1.3 Notice the creative way this season was organized around an Olympic theme with an international flavor.
Source: (D. Kahan, n.d.)

Sport Education seasons are longer than typical PE units because students have more to learn (e.g., techniques, tactics, refereeing, scorekeeping, and other roles) and it takes time for them to become competent game players (when their performance level is such that they enjoy the games, gain confidence, and want to learn and improve even more).

Affiliation

Students are members of teams and retain membership for at least the duration of a season. Some elementary programs (Darnell, 1994) have created teams that stay together in physical education for the entire school year. This yearly team affiliation allows a teacher to utilize recess and intramurals as extensions of the physical education program. The feature also allows teams in each class to compete for a year-long All-Sports Trophy. Much of the meaning derived from sport participation and a significant part of the personal growth that can result from good sport experiences are intimately related to affiliation; that is, being a member of a team that works together toward common goals.

> **W**e usually stay in our own little groups in PE. . . . in Sport Education we have to get along together so we have to know team members better.
>
> —Marianne, high school student, New Zealand

Team membership allows for the creation and assignment of roles within the team, so most students on a team for a given season will not only have the responsibility to contribute to team success as players, they will also have to perform responsibly as a statistician, manager, trainer, coach, or publicist. Team membership creates enthusiasm and support but will inevitably create problems among members of some teams. It is in working through these problems of relationships and responsibilities that children and youth grow and mature.

Formal Competition

Sport seasons are defined by schedules of competitions that are interspersed with practice sessions. The competition formats are varied, including dual meets, round-robin tournaments, and league schedules. (See chapter 6 for details on competition formats.) The schedule is often fixed at the start of the season, so teams can prepare appropriately. Practices gain meaning because they are preparation for real competitions that are known in advance. Games and contests are more meaningful because they are part of a full schedule. The entire experience leads to a culminating event that encourages students to be aware of their improvement as a team as well as the technical and tactical improvements they each must make to compete better.

Sport Education is done in seasons that move from early focus on practice and development to the seasonal schedule to the culminating event. As you will see, you can organize a seasonal schedule in various ways, and often the nature of the schedule depends on the particular sport you are using. For example, the gymnastics seasonal schedule will look quite different from the floor hockey seasonal schedule.

Culminating Event

It is in the nature of sport to identify which individuals and teams perform the best in a particular season. In collegiate and professional sport, events such as the NCAA Basketball finals, Super Bowl, and World Series become events of national importance. On a smaller scale, the culminating event of a Sport Education season can create similar excitement within a class and sometimes even for an entire school. Culminating events can also provide teams and players with the motivation to have their team be in the best possible position near the end of the season.

The formats for culminating events are quite diverse. They might be a two-day track and field competition, a 3v3 volleyball competition, a team gymnastics competition, or a round-robin softball tournament. The culminating event should be very festive and celebrate the successes of all the students and teams, as well as those teams that finished first in the competitions.

Record Keeping

Records come in many types: batting averages, shots on goal, assists, kills, times, distances, points per game, shooting averages, rebounds, and the like. They provide helpful feedback for players and teams. For example, if a record shows that a player's time in a sprint race has been reduced, the player can see that he or she has improved. And if records show that a basketball team has reduced turnovers and increased rebounds, the team can see that it has improved. Records also help players and teams develop new goals to achieve. In track and field, for example, early performances will help individuals and teams set goals to achieve lower times, longer distances, and higher heights. Records do not only provide scores and statistics; they can also be the results of judged performances, such as in gymnastics or skating. When records are kept and publicized, they serve to define standards for performance and can become an important part of the tradition of a sport. In Sport Education, students produce records by acting as scorekeepers and statisticians for contests during the season and, with experience, can act as judges.

In Sport Education, the team publicist and team statistician are responsible for maintaining, updating, and publicizing the team's performance records. Records provide teachers with an authentic form of student assessment. They also can be used to develop traditions within a school, such as the long jump record for fifth grade girls, the number of kills in 3v3 sand volleyball competitions for ninth graders, or the team record for defensive rebounds in seventh grade 3v3 basketball.

Festivity

The festive nature of sport can be seen everywhere in the world and at every level of sport, from the Super Bowl to the local Friday night high school game, from the pageantry of the Olympic Games to the state track and field finals, from soccer's World Cup to the Saturday afternoon youth soccer games on a community field. The festive nature of sport provides excitement and meaning for participants and adds an important social element to the experience. In Sport Education, teachers plan to make each season festive through a number of elements such as creating team names, colors, and pictures; regularly posting and giving attention to team and individual performances; celebrating fair play; and publicizing within the school for the Sport Education seasons. In one Midwest school, the physical education teacher produces a weekly highlight video from all the Sport Education classes. This "Sports Center—Plays of the Week" gets played on a continuous loop in the school's cafeteria, serving as a great advocacy tool.

The main features of sport—seasons, affiliation, formal schedules of competition, culminating events, records, and festive atmospheres—are hardly ever reproduced in physical education classes. This is why we believe that in many cases sport in physical education has been taught in ways that are incomplete and not authentic.

SPORT EDUCATION GOALS

14
Chapter Slides

What if boys and girls in a particular school system experienced a well-done Sport Education curriculum from third or fourth though twelfth grade? What might we expect to be the outcomes of these experiences as they graduated from high school and moved forward toward their adult lives? How well could they perform in the sport, dance, and exercise activities they learned in physical education? What would they know and value about those activities? How likely would they be to continue to participate in sport outside of school and beyond their school years? How able would they be to differentiate between good and bad sport practices in youth sport, school sport, or community sport? How likely would they be to work toward making sport better for children, youth, and adults by becoming more engaged in local sport organizations? The answers to these questions are clear in the ambitious **goals of Sport Education**: to educate students to be players in the fullest sense and to help them develop as competent, literate, and enthusiastic sportspersons.

1
Introduction to SE

A *competent* sportsperson has sufficient skills to participate in games and activities satisfactorily, understands and can execute strategies appropriate to the complexity of the activity, and is a knowledgeable games player. Competent students will learn to be comfortable and confident performing in increasingly complex forms of sports and other physical activities. Students cannot be comfortable and confident unless they know where to go, what to do, and how to anticipate the flow of events during activities so that they are in the right place at the right moment during the activity, and then have mastered the techniques to use at that moment to achieve the goals of the activity. Much of the problem of helping youngsters to build a commitment to lifelong activity is that so many of them never learn to be comfortable and confident in activities of any complexity.

A *literate* sportsperson understands and values the rules, rituals, and traditions of sports and activities and can distinguish between good and bad practices in those activities, whether in children's sport in a community or professional sport seen on television. A literate sportsperson is both a more able participant and a more discerning consumer, whether as participant, spectator, or fan. Becoming literate about sports and other activities is a prerequisite to helping ensure that sport and activity programs for children and youth are educationally sound and contribute to a safer, saner sport and activity culture.

> **A**lthough some students believed Sport Education was less effective in teaching isolated skills, all agreed that they learned more team strategies and how to apply skills in the game situation.
>
> —Carlson (1995a) p.7

An *enthusiastic* sportsperson participates and behaves in ways that preserve, protect, and enhance sport culture, whether it is a local youth sport culture or a national sport culture. Enthusiastic sportspersons want to continue to participate actively, because they have come to value the experiences and enjoyment derived from participation. Enthusiastic sportspersons also want to give back to a sport or activity so that the next generation can experience the joys and benefits of participation and the particular sport or activity can thrive and grow. When this goal is achieved with students in Sport Education, we should expect that they will become volunteers in child and youth sport ventures and take an active interest in seeing that sport is widely available to all in the community. One would also hope that these women and men who have had rich Sport Education experiences would be willing to step forward and speak out when they see sport practices that are contrary to the well-being of children and youth.

These goals are ambitious. They not only embrace the sport education of children and youth, but also have profound meaning for the health and vitality of the general sport and activity culture of a nation.

14
Chapter Slides

SPORT EDUCATION OBJECTIVES

Long-term goals are realized through regular and consistent achievement of shorter-term objectives. Sport Education objectives are achieved through the experiences students have during activity seasons. Thus, the following objectives would be pursued during each season of Sport Education.

• *Develop sport-specific techniques and fitness.* To learn to play volleyball well, students must learn to pass, set, spike, dig, and block. We refer to these actions as *techniques* (Launder, 2001). To play volleyball well, students also have to be able to move quickly, jump, and have a particular level of stamina. We refer to this ability as *fitness*. Specific technique and fitness objectives will differ depending on the sport season. For example, the techniques and fitness needed to learn to play soccer are different from those for volleyball. This objective is about doing the activity in its relevant context. In other words, students should have sufficient mastery of techniques to use them in the context of the game and have a sufficient level of fitness to both execute the techniques and persevere in the contest.

• *Appreciate and be able to execute sport-specific strategic play.* Traditional approaches to physical education have had a primary focus on techniques, but have been typically quite weak on tactics. *Tactics* are the strategies used by players and teams to gain advantage within a contest. In one research study (Romar, 1995) a teacher reported that the main objective of a basketball unit was for students to participate in a well-played game, but the practice sessions were all about dribbling, passing, shooting, and rebounding. Not a single practice task in the entire unit was focused on tactics. The games at the end of the unit showed the predictable result: Better players dominated, no discernible offensive or defensive tactics were shown, and students were often out of place and seemingly bewildered by the pace of play and movement of the ball. The teacher was disappointed. The game was a long way from being well played. In Sport Education tactics are as important as or more important than techniques. Students have to learn the basic tactics of play to understand what the game or activity is about. Nothing is more disheartening to learners in a game or contest than feeling that they do not know where to go or cannot anticipate the action so as to move to a position that allows them to participate and use their techniques. They feel out of place and awkward, and the result is that they are disappointed and even embarrassed to be in the contest. We refer to the combination of techniques and tactics for specific purposes in sport as *skill* (Launder, 2001).

• *Participate at a developmentally appropriate level.* In Sport Education, for various reasons, teachers hardly ever use the traditional parent game as played in formal competitive settings (such as soccer played on a regulation-sized field with 11 players to a side). They modify activities to allow students, at whatever developmental stage, to participate successfully while learning important techniques and tactics that will allow them to continue to develop in the activity. They typically modify the number of players on a side, the size of the court or field, the implements or balls, and the rules of the contest. For example, a teacher might use smaller or softer balls, shorter bats or sticks, nearer or lower targets, and larger goals to create a more developmentally friendly game in which students can have more success with techniques and gradually acquire a more sophisticated sense of tactics. Sport Education teachers also try to encourage continuous play by altering stop and start rules. Courts and playing fields are smaller, as is the size of teams. In volleyball and basketball, for example, nearly all techniques and tactics needed to play the adult form of those games can be learned in 3v3 contests. See chapter 5 for more information on game modifications.

Mind you, the fundamental nature of the game, its set of primary rules (Almond, 1986), is not changed. The primary rules of a game identify how the game is to be played and how winning is achieved. Volleyball is a striking game. The primary rule is, the ball is struck from one side such that the opponents on the other side of the net cannot return it successfully while it is still in bounds. Secondary rules, however, such as the size of the court and the height of a net or the size of a ball, can be changed without altering the primary nature of the game. Softball is a striking with implement, catching, and throwing game. Softball is a sector game played on a large, 90-degree sector space. Learning to play softball on a 90-degree sector field, students get very few opportunities to practice fielding, throwing, batting, and softball tactics. In this text you will learn ways of teaching basic softball skills and tactics in smaller-sector spaces so that you can multiply your students' opportunities to practice their skills and tactics and to produce faster-paced contests.

• *Share planning and administration of sport experiences.* In Sport Education students learn roles such as coach, manager, referee, statistician, trainer, and publicist. As students gain experience in the model, they participate more and more in the planning and administration of the program. In high schools, teachers often create a sports board where student members play a significant role in planning the seasons and adjudicating differences that might arise within and between teams. This objective produces two primary outcomes: ownership and empowerment. First, for students to develop and show a sense of ownership for the success of their own experience and that of their classmates, they have to develop a vested interest in making the season successful, and to gain that sense they must have responsibilities. Second, students will never become empowered to be literate and enthusiastic sportspersons without having the opportunity to experience significant responsibilities in their own sport education. When it becomes clear that the success of a team and the success of a season for a class depend on student responsibility in a number of roles, a built-in accountability system is created that helps students to take their roles seriously. In too many physical education programs, the only real responsibilities students have are to obey class rules and do what the teacher tells them to do. These conditions cannot help youngsters grow to be independent, responsible players and leaders in sport and physical activity.

> *What impressed me the most was when I asked the captains to come up with a drill, and they went home and made them up for their teams. As a result, we have a drill named after one child, called the Ricky drill, because it was such a great drill. Now every team does it.*
>
> —Middle school PE teacher, USA

• *Provide responsible leadership.* For Sport Education to achieve its several seasonal objectives, students must provide leadership within their teams; thus leadership becomes an objective also. This is particularly true, as you will see, for the roles of coach and manager. Coaches work with their teams to plan who will participate in various levels of competition, lead teams in warm-ups and technique practice, and help resolve any conflicts that might arise. Managers make sure that equipment is in the right place at the right time and that team members are at their appropriate assignments at the right time. For example, they make sure that team members who are referees and scorekeepers get to the right competition venue at the right time so that contests can begin on time. Not every student will be a coach or manager each season, but during the course of a school year every student will be asked to fulfill one or both of those roles. Teachers, therefore, must help students learn to be leaders by starting with small leadership tasks and then gradually broadening the roles as students develop leadership skills.

• *Work effectively within a group toward common goals.* In Sport Education, students are members of teams for each season. In most cases, team membership will change from season to season, but examples do exist where students stay on the same team for the semester or even an entire school year. A major outcome of the pedagogy of heterogeneous small learning groups is for students to learn to work together to achieve goals common to the group. The teams and seasons features of Sport Education create the context in which this objective can be achieved. Success in Sport Education is always team success. Teams cannot be successful unless each member of the team contributes; thus it is in the best interests of the team members to support each other and help each other be successful. Team camaraderie and spirit is promoted as teams create a name, a color, a team cheer, and other things that help build unity and make each student feel part of the larger effort. These features create the context within which teachers can emphasize effective team participation and individual students can be helped to learn the interpersonal skills necessary to be good team members.

> *I* have always been concerned about the social interaction aspect of phys ed and how you change the attitudes of boys and girls and their roles in sport. I have come to the conclusion that it doesn't work in a 1:30 ratio with the teacher dominating. You can change attitudes when students are working on things in a small team. This unit (Sport Education) has produced outcomes that I have been trying for years to produce in a normal situation.
>
> —High school PE teacher, New Zealand

• *Appreciate the rituals and conventions that give sports their unique meanings.* Part of truly learning a sport is coming to understand and appreciate its rituals and conventions. This objective underscores the intent of Sport Education to go beyond the techniques and tactics of playing a sport, to provide students with a broader understanding of the sport and how it is practiced in various places. Why are spectators quiet in golf and tennis but not in basketball? What do contestants typically do at the end of matches or contests? How do you show appreciation and respect to opponents and officials? Why is fair play fundamental to defining a good sport experience? These elements are all content for the sport educator.

• *Develop the capacity to make reasoned decisions about sport concerns.* Students' various responsibilities each require decision making. Inevitably, conflicts will arise within and between teams and those conflicts will have to be dealt with and resolved. As the season progresses tensions often heighten when teams compete to finish as high as they can in the standings. Because fair play is an integral part of Sport Education, concerns of what is fair and what is appropriate conduct arise throughout a season. All of these conflicts become teachable moments where students can be confronted with concerns that arise from their own sport experience. Students learn, with the help of their teacher, to deal with those concerns and resolve conflicts. Teachers can bring forward concerns to consider from other sport cultures, such as the local school sport culture or a local youth sport competition. In coming to grips with how a particular class can make their Sport Education seasons as fair and good as possible, students can also learn to distinguish between appropriate and inappropriate practices in other sport venues, thus becoming more literate about how sport practices, such as those in youth sport, sport clubs, and school sport, should be organized and implemented.

• *Develop and apply knowledge about umpiring, refereeing, and training.* Every student will umpire or referee during each sport season. Each season, one student on each team might play the role of trainer or fitness leader, becoming knowledge-able about and providing leadership in fitness training, injury prevention, and injury treatment. Most sport educators do not have to give rules tests anymore. Students who do not know the rules cannot referee or umpire well and the contestants will let them know that they are not applying the rules appropriately. This built-in accountability makes students take rules very seriously and they learn to make the right decisions in contests rather than just write a correct answer on a test paper; thus, their understanding of rules is more complete and authentic than if it is just cognitive content. Because all students referee or umpire in each season, the context is set for them to be more aware of how crucial good referees are to good competition and how difficult the tasks can be. This awareness may lead to students having a more balanced perspective, making them less likely to constantly criticize referees.

• *Become involved in sport after school and outside of school.* The primary goal most often cited for physical education today is to help students develop a commitment to lifelong physical activity. What students experience in their physical education program has to contribute to their wanting to become involved in activity programs outside of class, including having the knowledge about how and where to participate. Sport Education can contribute partially by making the physical education class an exciting and rewarding experience, one in which students master techniques and tactics to the point where they feel comfortable and confident in sport activities. That experience, however, is not enough. Sport Education teachers should also strive to help students learn where activities are done in their local communities and how they can become involved in those activities. For example, when students are introduced to volleyball they may be unaware of where youth and adults play volleyball in the community, how to access those opportunities, and what kinds of competitions are available. A Sport Education volleyball season should help them to learn about those opportunities in their own community.

14
Chapter Slides

DIFFERENCES FROM YOUTH, COMMUNITY, AND INTERSCHOLASTIC SPORT

Having described in the previous section how we have tried to make Sport Education more similar to authentic forms of sport, we now need to point out several important ways it differs from institutionalized forms of sport, such as youth sport, interscholastic sport, and elite sport. Sport Education differs from sport in communities and schools in three important ways: (1) participation requirements, (2) developmentally appropriate involvement, and (3) more diverse roles. These differences emphasize that Sport Education is not merely about learning a sport activity, but rather getting a more complete education in sport.

Participation Requirements

In Sport Education all students participate equally at all points in the season. Teams have no first string and second string. No players sit on the bench for a long time. This requirement alters the sizes of teams and the nature of the competitions. Sport Education favors small-sided games. Having large numbers of players on one side of a game usually means that more-skilled students dominate play and less-skilled students are much less involved (Siedentop, 1998). To learn the techniques and tactics of a sport, students must be involved repeatedly in executing techniques and tactics—it is that simple! To be involved repeatedly, they need small-sided teams with lots of action for each player.

This is also true for other parts of the Sport Education model. Culminating events should typically involve all the students—they are not all-star games. All students, not just the more gifted students or natural leaders, experience various roles in the season. Students who experience Sport Education realize quickly that all the players on the team must contribute for the team to be successful, creating the context within which team support and appreciation is fostered.

Developmentally Appropriate Involvement

The manner in which an activity is organized for Sport Education should be developmentally matched to the experiences and abilities of the students. Because time is limited and therefore quite valuable in physical education, participation must be arranged for students to get the most opportunity to learn techniques and tactics and other roles. Doing this always requires small-sided teams. We have found that 3v3 teams in volleyball and basketball allow students to learn all the important techniques and tactics, and dramatically increase the number of times they touch the ball. We have had success with elementary soccer seasons that start with 1v1 competitions emphasizing dribbling, tackling, and shooting, before moving to 2v2 and then 3v3, adding appropriate techniques and tactics with each new form of the game. For example, in the 2v2 game, we introduce passing and trapping and tandem defending. The full-sided adult forms of team games are hardly ever appropriate for Sport Education, simply because in 6v6 volleyball, 5v5 basketball, or 11v11 soccer some students will get many opportunities and others will get few.

The secondary rules of a game should also be changed while preserving the primary rules, or essence, of the game. Basketball is an invasion game emphasizing eye–hand coordination, moving the ball with dribbling and passing, and scoring by shooting. Secondary rules such as the size of the ball, height of the goal, or dimensions of the court can be altered to make the game more fun and easier to learn, as long as the primary rules are kept intact.

Diverse Roles

In most forms of youth and school sport, players learn only to be performers. In Sport Education, as we have described, they learn diverse roles that help them to better understand all the elements contributing to a successful sport experience. Indeed, in community and school sport, specialization is so common that players often learn to play only one position. For example, they may learn to be only a point guard, an outside hitter, or a shortstop. In Sport Education, students are more likely to learn to play multiple positions. And in learning to play other roles (refereeing, keeping score, compiling statistics, publicizing team performance, coaching, managing, or training), students also have the chance to see the sport from a much broader perspective, exposing them to and possibly preparing them for sport-related professions.

14

Chapter Slides

THE NATURE OF COMPETITION IN SPORT EDUCATION

Competition is fundamental to sport and to the sport experience. The term noncompetitive sport is a contradiction in terms. Physical educators worldwide have witnessed the abuses of inappropriate emphasis on competition in child and youth sport. Some volunteer coaches try to treat youngsters the way they see college or professional coaches treat their athletes. Coaches and even some parents try to convince the youngsters that a win-at-all-costs approach is the right approach. In youth sport, young participants sometimes see adults abuse the umpires or confront the volunteer coach as to why their youngster did not play more. We all know that those abuses are out there, even though we also know that good models of child and youth sport exist throughout the world. Because of abuses in community, youth, and school sport, some physical educators believe that too much competition exists and that physical education should not be competitive.

This problem needs to be addressed straightforwardly because it arises from legitimate concerns about the education and well-being of children and youth. What do youngsters most value about their sport participation? The evidence on this question has been consistent for many years (Siedentop, 2002). Children and youth want to get better at the sport, to be with their friends, and to have fun doing it. Winning and losing do not appear to be as important to them as they sometimes become to the adults that supervise and support them. Even when you listen to elite athletes talk about their competition experiences, you are as likely to hear about their hopes to perform well or up to their potential as about their wishes or expectations to win the competition.

We believe in the value of developmentally appropriate competition in Sport Education. In other words, you can learn important lessons from the study of what children enjoy and value when they organize informal, player-controlled games (Coakley, 1994). First, youngsters like action, especially action that leads to scoring. Second, they want personal involvement in the action—player-controlled games have no substitutes. Third, they want a close score, which means they want evenly matched sides. Fourth, they use games to reaffirm friendships and make new friends. Much of what we try to do in Sport Education aligns well with those values. We would add, of course, the creation of spaces, implements, and goals that make the game more friendly to the developing capabilities of the youngsters.

It is also worth noting that good competition is impossible without a substantial amount of cooperation among players. In dual and team sports, the cooperation necessary to perform and compete well is obvious. When you listen to the reactions of athletes to their competitive experiences, they are likely to mention the good lessons they learned about cooperation and camaraderie as they competed. What is most clear is that athletes at all levels resist and reject the notion of zero-sum competition, where one person or team can succeed only to the extent that the other person or team fails. Unfortunately, this view that winning is the most important thing, and that losing means you will have no satisfaction in having played your best or played fairly, is sometimes imposed on youngsters by adults in shamefully inappropriate ways.

It was a paradox. Winning had become more important than in regular physical education class. Judy (touch football) explained, "We really did want to win and it sort of nearly was everything because it was actually counting." This desire to win encouraged the higher skilled players to work with the less skilled, and the latter to work harder to improve. As the season progressed, however, while winning remained important, team improvement often became even more meaningful.

—Carlson (1995a) pp. 7-8.

Sport Education emphasizes the totality of the sport experience. Fair play is always important, not just in rhetoric but in point systems that determine seasonal champions and in recognition of exemplary fair play. Whether with third graders or twelfth graders, we believe that Sport Education emphasizes the *educative* values of the experiences. The evidence is compelling that appropriately organized and implemented Sport Education models demonstrate the characteristics of sport experiences that sport psychologist Mary Duquin (1988) suggested will nurture healthy physical, psychological, and emotional growth and development in children and youth. She suggested that the sport experience should

- be fun and enjoyable for participants,
- provide a safe means for developing activity skills,
- foster moral sensitivity and caring,
- realize the pleasure and beauty of movement skill,
- exercise a spirit of creativity, adventure, and discovery,
- provoke a commitment to lifelong involvement, and
- inspire a sense of community.

Experiences in Sport Education align well with these characteristics. Teams create small learning communities where caring and supporting are learned and practiced. Modified games create the conditions that enable learning of techniques and tactics. The emphasis on festivity creates fun and enjoyment in all the ways teachers help to make the seasonal experience special. Students act in a number of leadership roles, and teams make decisions that involve being creative and balancing risks and rewards. Together, these characteristics provide the best opportunity for influencing the emerging lifestyle choices that youth make.

We make no apologies for organizing competitions in sport, fitness activities, and dance activities. However, we do work very hard to make the competitive aspect of the experience contribute to the physical, social, and emotional development of the student. Sport Education is not about developing elite athletes; it is about educating children and youth in sport and other activities to help them become competent, literate, and enthusiastic about those activities.

GETTING STARTED IN SPORT EDUCATION

Chapter Slides

As you read through the following chapters, you will learn about the various ways to organize Sport Education. As you read this material, remember that you do not have to do everything we suggest can be done in implementing the model. In fact, we suggest that most first timers should do a very basic form of the model and then gradually add to its complexity. In the following chapters, we will advise you to first pick an activity that you know well and that your students are likely to enjoy. We will also advise you to adopt a basic format using teams and a scheduled season. We will then advise you to use only a few of the student roles, especially those that will help you do the season well, such as coach, manager, referee, scorekeeper, and publicist or statistician.

Planning Worksheets

Like any new approach to curriculum and instruction, it is important that your initial experiences be positive both for your students and for you as a teacher. Sport Education gets easier to implement as students learn to be comfortable in the model. Sport Education does require thorough planning and forethought about how to design such sport experiences. The accompanying CD-ROM includes several **planning worksheets** to help guide you through the preparation process. All the evidence supports the assertion that students will learn how to do their roles well and teachers will be more free to do the important teaching and interacting that lies at the heart of good learning. Start small. Do it well. Then build on it. That is our advice.

Chapter 2

Sport Education Curriculum and Instruction Strategies

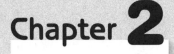

Sport Education is a curriculum and instruction model developed to allow students in physical education programs to have authentic, enjoyable learning experiences in sport, dance, and exercise activities. Sport Education is not business as usual; it differs in many ways from what students are typically expected to learn in physical education and how their teachers organize learning experiences. Most of all, the student roles in Sport Education are fundamentally different from roles students have in traditional approaches to curriculum and instruction in physical education. In this chapter we will discuss the foundations of the sport education curriculum and describe instructional strategies.

14
Chapter Slides

SPORT EDUCATION FOUNDATIONS

The curricular philosophy of Sport Education has two distinct features: (1) greater depth of coverage of content and (2) an expanded set of content goals. First, in Sport Education fewer activities are taught in a given school year, allowing students to learn each activity to a greater depth than is typical in multiactivity physical education programs. This less-is-more philosophy is consistent with current thinking in education reform. Most school curricula have been described by some researchers as a mile wide and an inch deep, an appropriate description for the multiactivity curriculum in physical education, where units are often as short as four to five class sessions. Students in multiactivity PE models often get a day of introduction, a day or two on basic skills, and then a day or two of doing the activity, before they move on to a new unit. Sport Education uses seasons, which are much longer units of activity. Seasons are designed to last long enough for students to learn and grow in the various outcomes and roles expected of them.

The second curricular feature of this model is that longer seasons allow teachers time to plan, organize, and achieve an expanded set of content goals. The content of typical physical education units focuses primarily and sometimes exclusively on skills, rules, and small bits of tactics. The content of Sport Education has a stronger focus on tactics and skills, but also includes learning about and practicing other roles important to how the activity is pursued outside schools,, such as coaching, refereeing, scorekeeping, compiling statistics, managing teams, publicizing results, and the like. Sport Education also takes seriously the need to help students understand and appreciate the rituals and conventions of various activities and to understand the differences between good and bad sport practices.

The instructional philosophy of Sport Education centers on developing and sustaining small, heterogeneous learning groups (Cohen, 1994) that we call teams. Within teams, students have various roles and responsibilities, all of which contribute to the team's successes. Within these small learning groups, students help and learn from each other. Sport Education instructional philosophy is also consistent with current research on effective instructional practices, referred to as contextual, student-centered (Alexander, Taggart, & Luckman, 1998), and situated (Kirk & Macdonald, 1998) learning models. None of this means that teachers should abdicate their responsibilities as instructional leaders. Rather, it means that they should fulfill these responsibilities using strategies that more fully engage and utilize the talents of students. As a result, students will become more responsible for contributing to effective classes and for achieving seasonal outcomes.

Teams learn, practice, and compete together. Competition is fundamental to the success of Sport Education. It provides motivation and enhances learning. The model also ensures that the competitions are fair and even and that all students understand that winning the competition is just one of several important outcomes. That is why Sport Education works for activities as diverse as basketball, orienteering, aerobic dance, cross-country skiing, table tennis, and Frisbee golf.

HOW SPORT EDUCATION FITS IN WITH CURRENT EDUCATIONAL THOUGHT

Sport Education is wholly consistent with current trends in curriculum and instruction in schools. In Australia it has been hailed as a student-centered approach to physical education (Alexander, Taggart, & Luckman, 1998) because it places students at the center of the learning process and gives them real responsibilities. It has been described as a good example of situated learning (Kirk & Macdonald, 1998; Kirk & Kinchin, 2003) because Sport Education learning experiences are highly contextual, so what students learn can be applied beyond the school experience.

In Sport Education student performances and competitions are public, so authentic assessment of them is easily available. Students play in basketball games where rebounds, shooting percentages, turnovers, and the like can be recorded. They do gymnastics routines that can be judged. They compete in archery where scores can be recorded. Teams perform folk dances where judges give them scores based on set criteria. In education assessment these are called exhibitions (Wiggins, 1993); that is, they are public performances where the actual performance leads to an authentic assessment. The fact that students perform and records are kept provides an ongoing authentic assessment that can be used to improve learning as well as recognize final accomplishments.

The small group learning that is central to Sport Education requires that team members cooperate on a number of tasks; thus, the model is consistent with various forms of cooperative learning. And, as in successful cooperative learning models, although team performance is an important outcome, each individual team member is held accountable for her or his contributions.

Sport Education is also consistent with the current emphasis on project-based learning. When students have to plan team strategies for a season, and the season is of sufficient length, the goal for the team to become as successful as possible becomes a project. In a project-based environment, learning is concrete rather than abstract. And rather than learn in isolation, students in Sport Education work and communicate with teammates to have a successful season.

Finally, many current scholars of education think that curriculum and instruction models should enable students to integrate knowledge and skills from various traditional school subjects. Integration is at the core of project-based learning. Sport Education offers many opportunities to integrate learning across subject areas, a goal that has become particularly important in middle school curricula. Chapter 11 includes extensive information on how to integrate academic subjects into Sport Education seasons.

ORGANIZING THE SPORT EDUCATION CURRICULUM

14
Chapter Slides

The feature of Sport Education that most affects how a curriculum is organized is the planning for seasons that are longer than typical physical education units. As we point out in several places, the emphasis in Sport Education is on depth of coverage and providing sufficient time for students to really improve during the season. The other important factor, of course, is the amount of curricular time assigned to physical education. Curricular time is determined both by the frequency of physical education classes—daily, once, twice, three, or four times per week—and the length of the class session, which might range from 30 minutes in a third grade class to two hours in a high school that uses a block-scheduling format for its curriculum. The accompanying CD-ROM includes several examples of **season block plans** that demonstrate the various season designs based on the school's scheduling format. We have always advised sport education teachers to err in the direction of planning for more rather than less time. As teachers we all tend to underestimate the time it takes students to master techniques and tactics and to learn to use them in well-played games. Following are two Sport Education curriculum design examples, one from the elementary level and one from the high school level.

8
Season Block Plans

Elementary Example

Darnell (1994) described an elementary curriculum in which the year started with a short fitness unit, followed by five sport education seasons. The PE program in her school operated on a four-day rotating schedule (i.e., every fourth day students participated in PE) and the classes were 50 minutes long. The length of each of the seasons was typically 12 class sessions. This meant that each season had a maximum of 600 class minutes and occupied a little more than 9 weeks of the actual school schedule. The fitness unit served two purposes. First, it allowed the teacher to get to know her students and to see them in various fitness activities, providing her with evidence pertinent to placing students on teams that would be as evenly matched as possible. Second, of course, it allowed her to introduce principles of fitness and learn the various fitness levels of the students.

The Sport Education curriculum included soccer, basketball, volleyball, gymnastics, and track and field. All of these are important international sports, but they each have different characteristics that, taken together, make for a coherent, balanced Sport Education curriculum (the rationale for which is described later in this chapter). This model has five Sport Education seasons each school year, each of which allows sufficient time for students to accomplish significant outcomes. In addition, the activities are repeated at subsequent grade levels, although not always in exactly the same form. Thus, the total amount of curricular time devoted to helping students become competent and confident in these activities is adequate to achieve the intended outcomes.

High School Example

Dugas (1994) described a high school physical education program where Sport Education was used as one element in the curriculum. Although physical education was required, this model allowed students to elect their PE classes. The school year was divided into four nine-week grading periods. The seasons were fall, early winter, late winter, and spring. Students could choose their activity from classes in three categories: Sport Education, recreation, or fitness (see table 2.1). The activities in the recreation and fitness offerings could easily be done using the Sport Education model, although they were not in this school.

Table 2.1   Yearly PE Activities in Three Areas

SPORT EDUCATION		
Racket sports	**Target sports**	**Team sports**
Badminton	Archery	Volleyball
Racquetball	Bowling	Track and field
Table tennis	Golf	Baseball
Tennis	Fencing	Softball
	Riflery	Cross country
		Soccer
FITNESS ACTIVITIES		
Weight training		
Aerobic dance		
Aerobic activities		
RECREATIONAL ACTIVITIES		
Swimming	**Recreational activities**	
Beginning swimming	Square and folk dancing	
Intermediate swimming	Backpacking and hiking	
Lifesaving	Recreational boating	

Adapted from S.E. Dugas 1994.

Within the Sport Education category, students could choose between team and individual sports (see table 2.2). An effort was made to have activities in the Sport Education category correspond to the availability of similar activities in the larger sport culture; that is, flag football and cross country in the fall, volleyball and soccer in the early winter, basketball and swimming in the late winter, and softball and track and field in the spring for the team sport offerings. Individual sport offerings included tennis, archery, fencing, badminton, golf, and table tennis. The length of these seasons is sufficient for students to accomplish significant improvement in techniques and tactics and for teams to learn to work together to achieve team goals.

Table 2.2   Seasonal Sport Education Schedule

Season	Team sports	Individual sports
Autumn	Flag football Cross country	Tennis Archery Table tennis
Early winter	Volleyball Soccer	Fencing Bowling Badminton Racquetball
Late winter	Basketball Swimming	Fencing Bowling Racquetball Riflery
Spring	Baseball Softball Track and field	Badminton Golf Archery

Determining Season Length

So, what is the appropriate length for a Sport Education season? In the national curriculum trial of Sport Education in Australian high schools, the recommended format was 20 class periods, two sessions a week for 10 weeks, resulting in four seasons each school year (SPARC, 1995). This format grew from the New Zealand national curriculum project in tenth grade physical education (Grant, 1992), where schools had to commit to having seasons lasting at least 20 class sessions to be involved in the trial. Thus, at least at the high school level, 20 class sessions has become the recommended norm (Mohr, Townsend, & Bulger, 2001).

While the Sport Education model needs no magic number of lessons to be applied, you need to consider a number of factors when planning the curriculum. You must of course have sufficient time in a season for students to learn the various roles, techniques, and tactics necessary for successful participation. Teams must have sufficient time to practice and compete. You should calculate season length based on the number of minutes per class and the number of classes per week, to determine how long (in weeks) the season will last. If PE is only scheduled one day a week for 45 minutes, it makes sense to have a season last for a full semester. If PE is scheduled every day for 50 minutes and the grading period is 9 or 10 weeks, then you could plan two seasons for each grading period using the 20-session model or one season lasting 40 class sessions.

The nature of the activity and the number of goals you have for student achievement can also help determine the length of a season. For example, if you want to do a Sport Education fitness season, you might choose to do it for an entire semester. Teams might have semester-long goals in cardiovascular fitness, strength, body composition, and flexibility. You would organize team competitions around reaching appropriate goals in each fitness category. You could attend to flexibility in each class session, with strength and aerobic goals the focus of alternate sessions. An 18- to 20-week semester season provides sufficient time to alter body composition, strength indexes, aerobic performance, and flexibility, each of which could comprise a separate team competition. On the other hand, a Sport Education Frisbee golf season might be considerably shorter because the techniques and tactics are fewer and can be learned quickly. The competition season of dual meets followed by a championship could be done in a fewer number of class sessions.

Dance suggests different attractive uses of time. Dance forms can indeed be done quite well in a Sport Education format. Richardson and Oslin (2003) described a series of three dance competitions within a nine-week season in which students met daily. The modern competition focused on solo performances within teams, the jazz competition focused on duets within teams, and the hip-hop competition focused on groups of 4 to 6 within teams.

Sport Education dance seasons can be of regular length or last an entire semester. If you focused on folk dance for a season, 20 to 23 class sessions would be adequate. If, however, you wanted to do more than one form of dance (folk, square, ballroom, stomp), it could easily take an entire semester with team champions in each of the dance forms and an overall semester champion. Many PE teachers, when first learning about Sport Education, suggest that their students would get bored by the long seasons. However, the many evaluations of Sport Education worldwide provide no evidence that students become bored. Quite to the contrary, their interest tends to grow as the season progresses.

14
Chapter Slides

DECIDING WHICH ACTIVITIES TO INCLUDE

Most U.S. school districts have a district course of study for each subject matter. This graded course of study typically includes objectives in several areas (e.g., knowledge, skill, personal development, fitness, and so on) followed by descriptions of the activities that can be taught in order to achieve those objectives. Decisions about which of those activities to include in the PE curriculum for a particular school level and school year depend on several factors, such as weather, facilities, and equipment. In larger school districts, teachers may be required to teach certain activities with decisions made at the district level rather than at the school level.

Rationale for an Elementary Curriculum Model

One can argue that at the elementary school level, children should experience a range of activities, each of which has a particular emphasis in terms of technical and tactical demands. Darnell (1994) described such a rationale for her elementary curriculum. As described earlier, the school year for third through fifth grades started with a fitness unit, used to assess student skills and fitness and to establish expectations for fitness that lasted throughout the school year. The bulk of the school year was comprised of five Sport Education seasons: soccer, basketball, volleyball, track and field, and gymnastics.

Soccer was chosen because it emphasizes manipulating an object with the feet. It is a field invasion game (like field hockey, all the football codes, lacrosse, and speedball) that requires offensive and defensive tactics, with frequent unpredictable changes from offense to defense and vice versa. It is also a highly active game with a strong cardiovascular component, and it can be played indoors or outdoors with little equipment. It is an important international sport that is becoming more widely available in U.S. community and recreational sport for children, youth, and adults.

Basketball was chosen because it emphasizes manipulating an object with the hands. It is a court invasion game (like team handball) with techniques and more patterned tactics than soccer. It too has frequent offensive and defensive changes. It is played widely in youth and adult recreational settings, and can be played indoors or outdoors with very little equipment. It is an important international sport that was invented in the United States.

Volleyball was chosen because it is a game of striking skills with the hands and arms. It is a court-divided game (like tennis and badminton) with techniques and tactics more predictable than for invasion games. It is played widely in recreational settings and is increasingly available to youth and adults. It can be played indoors or outdoors with little equipment. Variations such as beach volleyball have become increasingly popular. It too was developed in the United States.

Track and field was chosen because it caters to a wide variety of skills and interests. Some track and field events require speed, others require endurance, and still others require strength. The primary techniques are running, jumping, and throwing, all of which can be used by children in a variety of sport activities. Track and field allows for competitions against standards and previous best performances, as well as individual and team competitions. It can contribute to both cardiovascular and strength improvements. It is an important international sport.

Gymnastics was chosen because it emphasizes total body assembly and inversion. Upper body strength is required for several of the events. Gymnastics has a high aesthetic content and requires judging to determine performance outcomes. Gymnastic events require strength, balance, flexibility, and sometimes creativity. In many events the performance is a routine created by the competitor. The creation of routines allows students the opportunity to plan and create their own variations.

In the third through fifth grade model, the sport is repeated for three grade levels, allowing students to make substantial progress toward competence in that sport. The yearly progression, however, does not always have to be conceptualized as a repeat of the same form of the sport in the same situation. For example, in gymnastics, students could learn rhythmic gymnastics in one year, acrosport in the second year, and Olympic gymnastics in the third year. In volleyball, one year could be done outdoors as a version of beach volleyball. In soccer, one year could be done indoors in small spaces, while another could be done outdoors in larger spaces.

This example has shown a coherent logic for the selection of activities comprising a third through fifth grade elementary Sport Education program. At other levels and in other situations, you would use a different logic to select forms of sports and other activities. For example, for various reasons your Sport Education curriculum might include folk dance, aerobic dance, weightlifting, and orienteering. The point is that in Sport Education you can develop a customized curriculum with a logic to the choice of activities for a year and for an entire school program.

A Middle School Model

In the middle school, cross-curricular integration is often a significant element of how a curriculum is organized and taught. Sport Education offers tremendous opportunities for such curricular integration. Chapter 11 provides details about cross-curricular integration. Here, we will provide one example, that of an Olympic-themed model for Sport Education (Siedentop, 1994). In this variation of Sport Education, students are members of teams that each represent nations. This focus on global sport is enhanced if teams for a particular season represent nations from different continents. Students remain on their teams for at least one semester, so several seasons can be completed in various Olympic sports. The range of Olympic sports allows teachers to choose activities for which their space and equipment is adequate.

> *In health education, the outcome strands of human development and relationships worked in well with the team aspects of Sport Education. In art, they were designing posters, covers for their journals, and team sheets. In technology, on the computer, they were doing word processing linking to language, and much of the publicity was generated in this way, including writing information for the newsletter.*
>
> —Australian teacher, on integration through Sport Education

Teams adopt their nation's colors, flag, and national anthem. The music, art, poetry, and literature of the nation can be studied as homework and coordinated with the students' work in their other classes. An Olympic Committee can be chosen to govern the seasonal competitions within the semester. Representatives from each nation can form a committee to design and make Olympic awards as an art project. Students can study the sports of the nation they represent and learn about the nation's major sport heroes and heroines. They can also learn about the country's geography, food, music, and art. The opportunities for cross-curricular integration in the areas of social studies, literature, art, and music are substantial.

To enhance the Olympic theme and add to cross-curricular integration, each team can be required to understand and make their nation's flag and learn their national anthem. One student can be chosen to take the athlete's pledge, and another to take the official's pledge. Students can create representations of gold, silver, and bronze medals, which can be awarded for various individual and team performances depending on the sports competed. The entire experience can end with a festive closing ceremony.

High School Model Possibilities

In an ideal situation, a particular school district would have articulation among the elementary, middle, and high school physical education programs. Thus, selection of activities at the high school level would be influenced by what students had experienced at the earlier levels. High school physical education works best when students have options for choosing their activities. We do not suggest that PE should not be required, but rather that students be able to select activities from among those offered in any particular semester to fulfill the requirement.

As students grow older, differences in their sport skills and backgrounds tend to widen. If students do not have the opportunity to choose a particular activity, you should consider offering less familiar activities that tend to reduce these entering differences. With coeducational classes, gender is also a factor. Substantial evidence shows that girls are often marginalized in coeducational classes. One way to remedy this problem is to form coeducational teams but have multiple competitions; that is, a girls' competition, boys' competition, and coed competition. In tennis, for example, you could have girls' singles and doubles, boys' singles and doubles, and mixed doubles. In flag football, you could have separate boys' and girls' round-robin league tournaments, followed by a coed league tournament.

The high school model described earlier (Dugas, 1994) is one attractive way to organize an elective curriculum, but others exist also, such as the fitness example described earlier. Adventure activities lend themselves well to the small, heterogeneous learning group feature of Sport Education. Differences in requirements between states and between districts within states will tend to dictate the degrees of freedom physical education teachers have to plan Sport Education curricula at the high school level. We reiterate, however, our profound belief that elective programs are likely to be much more successful than programs where students are simply assigned to a PE class based on time available in their class schedule and with no knowledge about what activities will be available to them in that class.

SPORT EDUCATION AS SMALL GROUP LEARNING

Chapter Slides

The distinctive pedagogical feature of Sport Education is the centrality of mixed-ability small learning groups, which we call teams. Teams are sufficiently small—typically comprising 6 to 10 students—so that all team members can participate in team tasks. Students are expected to carry out their team and class tasks without their teacher's direct and immediate supervision (Cohen, 1994).

Research on small learning groups suggests that the following benefits are likely when this pedagogical model is used appropriately:

- Students have a stronger sense of control and ownership for their learning.
- Teachers are relieved of constant traffic cop–type duties.
- Time on task is increased, especially during dispersed practice.
- Peer support and pressure within teams serves as an accountability function.
- Students who tend to disengage are not left alone.
- It becomes more difficult for students to shy away from participation.
- Students learn to help each other—to give help and to accept it.
- All students contribute and no students dominate.

Group work within teams is an especially effective method for solving two problems that are common to teaching physical education: keeping all students engaged in team and class tasks, and providing relevant instruction and practice for students with widely varying abilities (Cohen, 1994).

Younger children and even older students who are not accustomed to the responsibilities of group work (and may have become very accustomed to being the passive recipient of teacher-led management, instruction, and practice) will require a transition period to move to the small learning group model. The initial tasks that teams are asked to perform should be small, and you should be prepared to assist students as they gain experience with this different instructional approach. Evidence shows that when students are moved immediately to small learning groups after experiencing only teacher-led instruction, the transition period might become chaotic. Many teachers in both the New Zealand and Australian national high school trials chose to make this move immediately rather than gradually and reported that classes were soon chaotic. However, they also reported that within several class sessions, the chaos disappeared and students were running the show responsibly. Several teachers thought this change was nothing short of miraculous. We believe that little can be learned from chaos; thus, we support the strategy of making a gradual transition.

The small learning group model is important for the students' personal and social development, which in turn contributes to the long-term goals of developing literate and enthusiastic sportspersons. Students first learn to become active citizens of their own team. They have responsibilities, and performing their roles well is essential to team success. Thus, the citizenship they learn is not individualistic, but rather related to the goals of the team. Students are required to plan and make decisions: Which team members will compete at the A, B, and C levels for this competition? Who will be the fitness leader for the season? Who will be the team publicist? What should the team publicist do? How can we do better in the next competition? Who is having problems refereeing and how can we help? To address these questions, students have to carry on an organized, focused discussion and they have to make decisions about their plans, then carry out those plans. These skills are essential for successful adults, but are too seldom practiced in school settings (Sharan & Sharan, 1992).

> **S**port Education is better than normal PE because the teachers weren't telling you what to do . . . you weren't under any pressure, and this made you want to try your best. You really learned how to cooperate with other team members and it was really good sharing the responsibility with each other.
>
> —Tenth grade student, Australia

Chapter Slides

KEY INSTRUCTIONAL FEATURES OF SPORT EDUCATION

Do not assume that teachers do no teaching in Sport Education. They do! The difference between Sport Education and PE is that teachers also act as educational engineers. By teaching students the appropriate class routines that ensure smooth management and by helping students to be successful in small, mixed-ability learning groups, teachers are actually designing a class environment within which important outcomes are more likely to occur. These outcomes include acts of personal and social responsibility that would be unlikely to occur in a class framework dominated by teacher-led instruction and practice. Most importantly, these outcomes are more likely to occur with students who are often unsuccessful and marginalized in physical education.

> • *Special needs students displayed unprecedented application to work within their roles in Sport Education.*
>
> • *Teachers suggested that the model favors lower-ability students and they significantly improved their motor skills as a result of increased participation.*

- *It appears that Sport Education is more gender inclusive than more traditional approaches to physical education.*

    —From Evaluation of the Sport Education II Project, SPARC, Perth, Western Australia.

Teachers using Sport Education have frequently reported that they actually do more individual teaching than in a traditional model. With students responsible for more of the management and leadership of warm-ups and technique practice, teachers can move about the space and work with small groups and individuals. Does this mean they never do whole-group, direct instruction? No.

Guided Practice

Whole-group direct instruction, or guided practice, is the appropriate teaching strategy in particular situations, such as when a new technique or tactic has to be introduced to a class (Siedentop & Tannehill, 2000). In this situation, you should be in a position to be seen by the entire class, and you should organize the class so that students can actually practice the technique or tactic. In this format, you introduce a technique such as the drop shot in badminton or one-handed shooting technique in basketball. Students then try to do the drop shot as you showed them (even if it is a shadow response without hitting the shuttlecock). Your goal in this situation is to see that all students understand the main technical features of the shot, what we call the critical elements. You point out common errors so students can learn to discriminate between the critical elements and common errors. As students practice, you correct major errors in performance and reteach the technique.

The same would be true for a particular tactic, such as the back-door cut in basketball: With students gathered centrally, you explain the context for and execution of the back-door cut, giving students the opportunity to ask questions. You organize students so they can do a walk-through of the maneuver. The goal of guided practice is to get students to the point where they can benefit from independent practice that will be led by coaches. While independent practice is crucial for technique development, guided practice is necessary to ensure that students will not make major technique or tactical errors when they are dispersed to their team practice sites.

Combinations of techniques can and should be practiced together. For example, when providing guided practice for free-throw shooting, you can also teach the techniques of boxing out and rebounding. The following independent practice can be a free-throw game in which points are scored both for making a free throw and boxing out and rebounding missed free throws.

Independent Practice

In independent practice, the team should practice techniques and tactics in its home space, led by the student coach. You should carefully explain the organization for practice before dispersing students. Posters showing the critical elements and common errors of the technique or tactic are very helpful. It is in team practice that students learn to work together and to help one another. While the coach provides the primary leadership for practice sessions, you make it clear that students are meant to help each other. Students who understand and grasp the technique or tactic quickly should provide assistance to teammates who are having trouble. You should emphasize teammates helping one another, then recognize and support it when you see it occurring. During practice, you move about the entire class space and offer feedback, assistance, and support.

> **D**uring the practices I can work with kids who maybe need a little help to improve their ability level without interfering with the rest of the group. I can teach one kid while the others are developing their skills instead of teaching them skills they don't all need.
>
> —Seventh grade teacher, Australia

Sport Education research provides convincing evidence that students like and appreciate this small group learning model. At the outset, you should supervise independent practice to ensure that the teams are practicing appropriately. The more experience students have with the model, the better they are able to work within it and profit from it; thus, you should expect that across multiple seasons and years in Sport Education students will become quite good at the give and take that characterizes small group learning. As student capacity to work within the team concept improves, you do less supervision and more teaching assistance during team practice.

Chapter Slides 14

HELPING STUDENTS DEVELOP GAMES SENSE

Students enjoy games and activities to the extent that they feel comfortable in the flow of play. Soccer games where students swarm to the ball are not enjoyable except perhaps for the most skilled students. Basketball games where the flow of play is helter-skelter and the ball is dominated by the most-skilled players are not fun for most participants. Volleyball games where 90 percent of the points are scored on serves that cannot be returned are not fun for anybody. As we have said repeatedly, traditional PE instruction has a strong focus on skills (what we will call techniques) and not nearly as much emphasis on game tactics. In Sport Education the primary focus is on developing games sense (Launder, 2001). At its essence, games sense is understanding in action. Its simplest meaning is that "players get into the best possible position at the right time and make sensible decisions about what to do next" (Launder, 2001, p. 36). (We are grateful for the rich and creative work done by Alan Launder and described at length in his book, *Play Practice: The Games Approach to Teaching and Coaching Sports.* The material in this section draws heavily on that book, and we recommend it to all teachers who want to develop Sport Education programs.)

Games sense is a combination of learning appropriate techniques, applying tactics, and understanding rules. We agree with Launder (2001) that this combination is properly called skill; thus, the skilled player is one who understands the flow of a game, knows the tactics the team is trying to execute, gets in the right position, makes good decisions, and has the techniques to execute the decisions. We use the term *techniques* to describe what are traditionally referred to as skills; that is, dribbling, backhand striking, jump shooting, heading, digging, fosbury flop, or handstand. The balance of time devoted to practicing techniques or tactics depends on the sport or activity.

In some sports, such as the field events in track and field or the balance beam or parallel bars in gymnastics, technique practice will dominate preparation. Tactics will come into play when students are required to plan their own routines. In target games, such as archery and bowling, technique practice will dominate while tactics take a minor role. In sector games, such as softball or cricket, techniques are crucial to success, but tactics become important. In court-divided games, such as volleyball, tennis, or badminton, techniques and tactics are more evenly balanced. In invasion games, such as basketball, hockey, and all the codes of football, tactics become as important as or more important than techniques. For example, in most invasion games, such as soccer or basketball, the actions of players off the ball are critical to the success of the team. These actions require an understanding of the flow of the game and a mastery of the team's tactical goals. They do not require any specific techniques (such as dribbling, shooting, or passing). Thus, the development of games sense in invasion games has a strong focus on tactics.

Technique Practice

You should organize practice for technique mastery in ways that are as close to the context of performance as possible. Practicing techniques with isolated drills makes the transfer of the technique to the competitive situation difficult, especially for activities where tactics become more important. For example, techniques in softball, volleyball, and hockey all require using the techniques in fluid game situations where flexible responses are required for success. Isolated drills tend to produce only stereotyped responses and are less useful. Drills, therefore, should be as gamelike as possible.

The key to improvement in practicing techniques is successful repetitions. You should organize and manage your class in a way that allows optimum time for practice. Students need to understand how a technique fits into the overall pattern of the activity. You should organize them into the smallest group that is consistent with achieving the objectives of the practice task. With a team size of 6 to 10 students, this usually means that you can organize 2 to 5 practice groups within each team. Practice tasks should always have a goal that is challenging, and students should be able to see and judge the results of their efforts. Practice tasks should have sufficient variation around a technical theme (e.g., passing and setting in volleyball) and should follow an obvious progression.

Technical practice is obviously enhanced when sufficient space, equipment, and time are available. You should modify tasks so that the techniques being practiced are those that approximate the mature technique played in a regular game. This is difficult to do if the equipment is not also modified. For example, when children learn to shoot in basketball, you might follow all advice for technical instruction, but if the ball is regulation size and the basket is 10 feet high, then little appropriate technical development will occur; indeed, students will be most likely to learn inappropriate shooting techniques.

In activities where tactics are important, technique practice should incorporate the appropriate tactical emphasis to provide the richest context for practice. Tactics often involve using techniques in chains (a sequence of maneuvers that are linked together to achieve a goal). For example, the fast break in basketball requires rebounding, passing, dribbling, more passing, and then shooting, with off-the-ball players' movement particularly important. In volleyball, the sequence of passing, setting, and spiking can be practiced as students' abilities increase. In many cases, practicing these chains of techniques and tactics from back to front rather than vice versa provides great benefit. Fast-break practice can start with the lay-up, then proceed backward to add passing, dribbling, passing, and rebounding, along with off-the-ball movement. The benefit of this backward chaining strategy is that the intended outcome (the successful shot in basketball or the successful spike in volleyball) gets the most practice attempts. This approach also provides the most fun for the players, because they achieve the successful culmination of the sequence more frequently.

Tactical Practice for Invasion Games

In invasion games the understanding and practice of tactics becomes crucial to developing games sense. In invasion games, one player controls the ball, while all his or her teammates move to get in position to execute a tactical strategy. For all players, time on the ball is only a small fraction of their time off the ball, especially in games where the player–ball ratio is high, such as all the football codes (soccer, rugby, American football) (Launder, 2001). Tactics in invasion games are those strategies through which "attackers combine with teammates to keep possession of the ball and try to score, as well as the way in which defenders maneuver to regain the ball" (Launder, 2001, p. 37).

Attacking tactics in invasion games are designed to create situations where offensive players outnumber defensive players at the right time and the right place. These tactics involve the following principles:

- Players create space by moving into good positions at the right time.
- This action creates time because defenders must take time to close the distance.
- Attackers use this space and time to be skillful (make decisions and execute techniques).
- Receivers should indicate where the ball is to be delivered and scan play as the ball is received.
- Attackers then decide what to do next—shoot, pass, or run (dribble).
- In continued passing, the passer must select the best possible receiver.
- The pass should be delivered to the right spot at the right speed for the receiver.
- At all times, attackers should maintain floor or field balance.

Defender tactics are designed to prevent scoring, to regain the ball, and to make the transition to effective attacking play. These tactics involve the following principles:

- Respond immediately to change of possession from attack to defend.
- Always keep pressure on the ball.
- Provide coverage for the defender who is pressuring the ball.
- Try to deny off-the-ball attackers from moving into advantageous positions.
- Closely guard attackers who occupy important spaces.

Practice tasks to teach and develop tactical awareness typically involve uneven sides; that is, 3v1, 3v2, 4v3, and the like. Uneven-sided practice tasks can have the purpose of maintaining possession (possession games) or scoring (go-for-goal games) (Launder, 2001). You can organize these so that they flow continuously rather than experience multiple stop-starts, thus optimizing the time spent in actual practice. Examples of uneven-sided practice tasks and mini-games are available in the accompanying CD-ROM.

Techniques and Tactics Practice for Court-Divided Games

Techniques and tactics are more balanced in their importance in court-divided games, such as volleyball, tennis, badminton, and table tennis. Tactics in court-divided games are more programmed than in invasion games where the flow of play is less predictable. We will use volleyball as our example. Volleyball is a hit game, not a catch-and-throw game. The key technical elements are the forearm pass, overhead pass, spike, block, dig, dink, and serve. The excitement of volleyball is heightened when players keep the ball in play through rallies of retrieving and returning. This makes controlling the ball and passing the most important skills, rather than blocking and spiking. As students improve in their capacity to control the ball, they can begin to focus on the positioning of opponents so as to direct the ball to the opponent's weaknesses.

Techniques in volleyball are often sequentially dependent—pass, set, spike (Launder, 2001). Technique development practice should be as gamelike as possible. Volleyball is a game of angles and redirection, so you should create practice drills that replicate what will be used in the game setting, usually involving three players, with one teammate as a retriever and one player as a feeder. The tactics and techniques that are most important are as follows:

- Setting up to attack—on-the-ball techniques
  - Serve
  - Forearm and overhead pass
  - Spike
- Setting up to attack—off-the-ball play
  - Open up (move to unobstructed space)
  - Transition to new position
  - Back up teammates (support)
- Defending—on-the-ball techniques
  - Dig
  - Block
- Defending—off-the-ball play
  - Base position
  - Pursuit
  - Open up
  - Transition

Volleyball practice is best done in triads; indeed, a 3v3 competition is often the best organization to ensure optimum opportunity and excitement. USA Volleyball uses the term Try-angles as a teaching tool to promote this understanding. A commonality among all court-divided games is that you typically do not send the ball back in the direction it came from; that is, you try to change angles.

Games sense is most easily developed when the court and equipment are modified. (See chapter 5 for a full discussion of game modifications.) A key element to early practice and competition is starting with a free ball rather than with a serve. A free ball is an underhand pass over the net to start the action. It should be used until passing techniques are fairly well developed.

Students best learn volleyball techniques and games sense if the action of the ball is slowed down and the ball is softer when hit. Many students have difficulty learning passing and setting techniques because they are not in the correct position to execute the technique. Slowing down the ball and emphasizing moving to intercept the ball will better allow learners opportunities to intercept and redirect the ball appropriately. You can provide these opportunities in several ways: by raising the net, using a lighter ball that floats longer, and using a reduced court area. Early scrimmages and practice games should focus on keeping the ball in play through cooperative scoring, where the two teams try to keep the ball going over the net as many times as possible. As players improve in their techniques and show evidence of developing games sense, you can introduce a scoring game as an initial competition with a free ball and a net height that is set at about the average height that players can reach standing on the tips of their toes (Launder, 2001).

Chapter Slides

DEVELOPING KNOWLEDGEABLE GAMES PLAYERS

Games sense is the crucial element in developing knowledgeable games-players. When students begin to feel comfortable in the game setting, when they know how to anticipate the action, and when they have sufficient command of the techniques to use in each situation, the game becomes both more fun and more challenging. As students in Sport Education grow toward those goals, you should create opportunities for them to think about and make decisions about various aspects of team practice and competition. For example, having each player on each team create a drill for a particular technique or combination of technique and tactic will get students to think about the game and how practice can improve performance. Requiring teams in a 3v3 basketball competition to choose between a person-to-person defense and a zone defense for a particular round-robin tournament, and then to work together to develop an offense based on the defensive choices teams have made, creates the context for teams to think about, discuss, and choose a particular tactical approach. It is also likely to create a sense of ownership among teammates for the team's decisions and performance. And, these students will be more likely to become knowledgeable basketball players.

> **Y**ou have to organize it yourself . . . We (team) were sort of independent from the rest of the class . . . I have played team sports before, but now I feel more confident about learning a sport.
>
> —High school student, New Zealand

Knowledgeable games players are unlikely to develop if students simply follow your directions. Creating contextual situations in which students have to think about and weigh options for defending and attacking will greatly aid in developing their understanding of tactics. Creating situations in which teams design their own practices based on team goals will surely increase students' involvement in and ownership of their team's performance. These are not instructional strategies to use the first time you try Sport Education or with students who have little background with a particular sport or activity. They are, however, useful strategies to employ as students grow more experienced with Sport Education and with the chosen sport or activity.

CUSTOMIZING SPORT EDUCATION TO FIT SCHOOL GOALS

Chapter Slides

You can adapt Sport Education to meet particular teacher or curriculum goals. A good example of this type of adaptation is the work done over a five-year period at the Columbus School for Girls (CSG). In the middle school PE curriculum students get introduced gradually to a variety of roles (see table 2.3 for a sequence of how roles develop throughout the curriculum) and what it means to be part of a team and have responsibilities that help the team and season to be successful. In the ninth and tenth grade, the entire PE curriculum is done using the Sport Education model. Each season lasts seven to eight double periods. Students are on teams for the duration of each season. The roles of coach, referee, trainer, publicist, manager, captain, statistician, and scorekeeper are used for each season. Each of the ninth and tenth grade years has six activities; the ninth grade activities are very sport oriented (such as field hockey, lacrosse, and basketball) and the tenth grade activities move to more of a lifetime activity focus (such as volleyball, dance, weightlifting, and table tennis).

So far that description sounds fairly typical of a Sport Education model used extensively by all teachers in a PE program. But CSG believes that girls should develop as strong, independent leaders who learn to make reasoned decisions and work together for a common good. This is a goal throughout the CSG curriculum, not only in PE. For example, in the coach role, students in sixth and seventh grades learn to lead the team, give pep talks, and arrange for all girls to play equal time. In the eighth grade, they do all those things, plus they have a role in designing the nature of the competition for the season. In the ninth and tenth grades, the coaches from each of the teams work together to create and design the competition for the season, teach skills, organize and lead drills, and make decisions (with team input) on how the team will organize the various levels of competition in a season. Indeed, each of the roles in the ninth and tenth grades is filled with important responsibilities. For example, the student referees decide what the rules will be and what the penalties will be for rule violations.

This chapter has shown that the Sport Education model has implications for both the planning of curriculum and the variety of teaching and learning experiences used in classes. The evidence is persuasive that students respond well to both the curricular features of Sport Education and the kinds of learning experiences they have in their small learning groups, or teams.

Table 2.3   How Roles Develop Throughout the Curriculum

Team role	6th-7th grade	8th grade	9th-10th grade
Coach	Lead team, give pep talks. Ensure that all team members play.	Lead team, give pep talks. Ensure that all team members play. Design tournament.	Lead team, give pep talks. Ensure that all team members play. Design tournament. Teach skills and drills. Teach positions. Organize players for teams.
Captain	Lead on field, motivate. Set good example.	Lead on field, motivate. Set good example.	Lead on field, motivate. Set good example. Organize team for games. Settle disputes.
Manager	Set up equipment. Clean up equipment.	Set up equipment. Clean up equipment.	Set up equipment. Clean up equipment. List equipment needed.
Trainer	Lead fitness sessions.	Lead fitness sessions.	Lead fitness sessions. Teach injury prevention. Treat injuries. Provide water. Take care of medical kit.
Publicist	Announce contests. Advertise game results. Post sport-related news.	Announce contests. Advertise game results. Post sport-related news.	Announce contests. Advertise game results. Post sport-related news. Make seasonal awards.
Statistician	Keep stats during games.	Keep stats during games.	Keep stats during games. Make up stat sheet. Provide stats to coach. Give results to publicist.
Scorekeeper	Keep score during games. Keep time.	Keep score during games. Keep time.	Keep score during games. Keep time. Track substitutions. Know the rules. Manage all aspects of games.
Referee	Referee games.	Referee games.	Referee games. Teach rules. Modify rules to fit games.

Chapter 3

Defining Student Roles

One of the main goals of Sport Education is for students to share in the planning and administration of their sport experiences. To accomplish this goal, Sport Education teachers create a variety of **student roles** for each season. When students get to learn and perform in a variety of roles other than the player role, they feel more responsible for their own participation and the success of the team, and they can contribute to the overall success of the season. The purpose of this chapter is to describe those roles.

14
Chapter Slides

3
Student Roles

PRIMARY STUDENT ROLES

In contrast to interschool competitions or recreational leagues, during Sport Education students perform in a host of roles other than just player or performer. Students learn to be coaches, referees, and scorekeepers. Further, in many sport education variations, they also learn to be managers, publicists, statisticians, and trainers. In one example from Australia, where seventh grade students competed in a modified form of Aussie Rules football, the role of sideline cameraman was added. The student cameraman followed play with a small camcorder and provided live commentary. The tape could be played back within class, and students could borrow the tape to share it with parents and friends. The roles created for students in Sport Education typically depend on the students' ages, their previous experiences in Sport Education, and their teacher's creativity. This use of roles contributes to a more complete understanding of sport and hence a more literate sports player. The learning and practicing of roles may even contribute as a form of career education for sport-related professions.

Students report that they enjoy taking these nonplaying roles and take them seriously. Although some off-field chores are seen as more exciting than others (e.g., refereeing is seen by some as more attractive than equipment manager), studies have also shown that students show particularly high levels of commitment to these roles. Although the specific nature of roles differs from situation to situation, we have chosen to list four categories of roles: player, required duty team roles, team roles, and specialist roles.

Player

Player is the most important role. Actively taking the role of player means making a significant contribution to one's team and to the competition. This role involves making an effort to learn techniques and tactics, playing hard and fairly, supporting teammates, and respecting opponents and officials. Remember that in Sport Education all students get equal opportunity to play and how well they play contributes to the overall success of the team; that is, the play of less-skilled students in a graded competition counts equally to the play of more-skilled students.

Required Duty Team Roles

All students occupy certain roles each Sport Education season and on each competition day. Apart from player, these roles are, at a minimum, referee and scorekeeper. By *required*, we also mean that *all* students have to learn to do these roles well in that season. So, you will need to plan time and strategies that allow students to learn and practice these roles. Duty team students also have important tasks in ensuring that contests start on time and that equipment is in place for them to do so. In many Sport Education variations, the role of team manager is also considered to be a duty team role. But unlike referee and scorekeeper, roles done by all students, each team has one manager in charge of seeing that equipment, referees, and scorekeepers get to assigned spaces quickly.

Team Roles

Team roles are nonplaying roles that serve to promote the functioning of an individual team. All teams involved in a season will have students occupying these roles, which include coach, manager, fitness specialist, and trainer. The choice for a teacher is how many of these roles to include in the Sport Education season. Typically, more roles are added as students and their teacher gain experience with the Sport Education model. For example, you should review the Columbus School for Girls (CSG) sequential model for introducing roles in the Sport Education curriculum (see chapter 2, p. 33) to see how one school introduces roles and increases the responsibility in those roles across grade levels.

Specialist Roles

You should endeavor to have one role other than player for each player in a team. In some seasons, you may choose to have students involved in one duty team role and one role not directly related to competition. These roles include special roles that may be specific to a sport, such as line judge in tennis or hurdles marshal in track and field. Still others relate to the marketing and promotion of the season itself, such as publicist, photographer, broadcaster, or newsletter editor.

Many other roles are available for incorporating into a Sport Education season. This category of specialist roles is virtually endless, and limited only by your imagination. In fact, any activity associated with a given sport (either from an officiating, broadcasting, or administrative perspective) has a legitimate place. For example, a swimming season may incorporate starters, timekeepers, and lane judges as officials, an announcer and commentator in broadcast roles, and an event manager and scoreboard operator in administrative roles.

Table 3.1 contains detailed descriptions of those roles required of all players in every Sport Education season. Table 3.2 contains an extensive number of roles available that relate to a student's team or to a specific sport. Some roles, such as coach and manager, are filled each day throughout the season, while other roles, such as referee and scorekeeper, are filled only when the team is assigned as duty team.

*I*n one Australian setting, students studied turf grass management in conjunction with their cricket season. In addition to preparing the playing field, the role of groundskeeper (more correctly, curator) by necessity also involved students in the daily ritual of collecting the dog droppings that accumulated in the popular park where classes took place. What is more, these droppings were used in the fertilizer experiments related to grass management that the students conducted in science class.

Table 3.1   Required Student Roles

PLAYING ROLE	
Role	**Responsibilities**
Player	Give a good effort in trying to learn techniques and tactics. Play hard and fairly. Support teammates. Respect opponents and officials.
REQUIRED DUTY TEAM ROLES	
Referee	Manage the contest. Make rule decisions. Keep the contest moving without undue influence.
Scorekeeper	Record scoring performance as it occurs. Keep a running account of the status of the ongoing competition. Compile scores. Turn over final records to the appropriate person (teacher, publicist, manager, or statistician).

Table 3.2   Optional Team and Other Specialist Roles

TEAM ROLES	
Role	**Responsibilities**
Coach	Provide general team leadership. Direct skill and strategy practice. Help make decisions about lineups. Turn in lineups to teachers or manager.
Captain	Represent the team on the field in conversations with officials. Provide leadership during play. Assist and encourage teammates.
Manager	Assume the administrative functions of ongoing team responsibilities. Turn in appropriate forms. Help get team members to the right locations for their roles as performers, referees, scorekeepers, and the like.

(continued)

Table 3.2 *(continued)*

TEAM ROLES	
Role	**Responsibilities**
Equipment manager	Collect and return team equipment. Collect and return playing jerseys. Inform teacher of any equipment loss or damage.
Fitness specialist	Lead team warm-ups. Provide leadership in a team's fitness schedule.
Trainer	Know common injuries associated with a sport. Access first-aid materials when requested. Notify the teacher of any injury during practice or competition. Aid teacher in administration of first aid and in subsequent rehabilitation.
Publicist	Compile records and statistics and publicize them. Contribute to the weekly sport sheets, school newspaper, posters, or a specially created sport education newsletter.
Journalist	Write match reports. Submit seasonal reports to the publicist or other advocacy agency (e.g., teacher, school administration).
Commentator	Introduce players before competition. Describe play during competition.
SPECIALIST ROLES FOR INVASION GAMES (SOCCER, BASKETBALL, FLAG FOOTBALL)	
Timekeeper	Know the rules concerning starting and stopping the clock. Operate the clock as designated by the referee. Clearly indicate the end of playing periods.
Statistician	Record pertinent performance data. Compile complete data. Summarize data across competitions. Turn the summarized data over to the appropriate person (teacher, publicist, or manager).
Ball retriever	Keep up with the flow of play. Supply replacement balls for those that go out of bounds. Retrieve out-of-play balls.
Down markers (flag football)	Clearly place down markers at appropriate positions. Move down markers at appropriate times. Display downs clearly to referee and players. Change down numbers on indicator boards.
SPECIALIST ROLES FOR TARGET GAMES (ARCHERY, BOWLING, GOLF)	
Target judge	Determine specific point values of shots. Signal point values to scorekeeper. Signal when target is ready for resumption of shooting.
Pin restacker/ball returner	Replace struck pins to appropriate positions. Return balls to throwing or rolling area.
Safety judge	Make sure participants are behind the shooting line. Determine when participants may resume shooting.
Course marshal (golf)	Manage flow of play between holes. Locate balls that may have gone off course. Clearly mark lost balls when located.

SPECIALIST ROLES FOR PERFORMANCE SPORTS (GYMNASTICS, DANCE, AEROBICS)	
Role	**Responsibilities**
Choreographer	Know requirements of compulsory and optional skills. Design movement sequences for team members. Help teammates learn sequence links. Record sequences for submission to judges or scorekeepers. Help select appropriate music.
Music engineer	Check and operate the sound system. Record music team members will use during their sequences. Play team members' music during practice and competition.
Property manager	Store and distribute props used by team during performances. Design and construct team props and costumes.
Judge	Score participants' performances. Know criteria for routines. Be able to justify scores according to set criteria.
SPECIALIST ROLES FOR RACING SPORTS (TRACK EVENTS, CROSS COUNTRY RUNNING, CROSS-COUNTRY SKIING)	
Starter	Summon racers to start positions. Give clear preparation signals. Signal start of races. Judge for false starts and breaks.
Timekeeper	Know how to use a stopwatch. Record racers' scores of athletes for relevant times. Turn over racers' times to the appropriate person (teachers, coach, manager, scorekeeper, or statistician).
Place judge	Determine winners and place getters from races. Consult timekeepers where races involve close finishes. Report places to scorekeeper.
Course marshal	Help racers stay on the designated course. Report lane or area violations to referee. Give progress times to athletes. Judge legality of transitions in relays.
SPECIALIST ROLES FOR STRENGTH SPORTS (WEIGHTLIFTING)	
Judge	Judge legality of the lift. Assign point values where appropriate.
Spotter/weight loader	Ensure safety of weightlifter by assisting where necessary. Load and unload appropriate weight onto the bar. Replace weights in designated areas.

A NOTE ON REFEREEING

In many sport education seasons, the quality of student refereeing will go a long way to determining the quality of the season as a whole. It is critical then, that you give students chances to practice this role before scheduling the games of consequence, and that you help all students understand that the primary role of the referee is to keep the game moving forward smoothly.

Modifying the rules is a particularly helpful way of assisting beginning referees, because they have fewer decisions to make. For example, to restart play in soccer, you may allow students to kick or throw the ball to their teammates (using any form of throw), rather than limit them to the specific throwing technique seen in competitive soccer. Nevertheless, as you modify games, you can make refereeing more complex. As games become more complex, more rules need to be enforced. However, these modifications typically occur as students have developed some beginning refereeing skill, or when they have experience with a particular activity in Sport Education. Table 3.3 provides a learning sequence of five stages for helping students to become good referees.

Table 3.3 Helping Students Become Good Officials

Level	Basketball	Volleyball or softball
Stage 1: Being a player	The student is a player in the game.	The student is a player in the game.
Stage 2: Following the teacher	The student moves with the teacher and learns about the positions on the court and about following the ball.	The student stands behind the teacher and learns to make the correct judgments and signals. For base umpiring, the student takes the correct position according to the base runners and moves according to where the ball is hit.
Stage 3: Assistant official	The teacher is still lead official, but the student indicates fouls and other decisions.	The teacher makes the call, and the student makes the appropriate signal.
Stage 4: Co-officials	The teacher assumes a backup role.	The student tells the teacher the decision, and the teacher stops the game if the decision is correct. The student then makes the appropriate signal.
Stage 5: Student officials	The teacher takes no official role.	The teacher takes no official role.

Reprinted, by permission, from P. A. Hastie, 1998, "Helping middle school students become good officials," *Journal of Teaching Elementary Physical Education,* 9(4): 20-21.

Teachers often use preseason scrimmages to help students practice the skills of refereeing and scorekeeping. Class time can also be devoted to showing students what rules are most likely to be broken and what kinds of fouls are most likely to occur and how they should respond to them. When students perform well in these roles, they need to be recognized and given positive feedback.

14
Chapter Slides

CHOOSING ROLES FOR A SEASON

Whichever roles you chose for a Sport Education season, consider these five major factors:

1. You must clearly define the roles you choose.
2. Your season plan should include specific time to help train students in the roles they will be performing.

3. Students need practice performing these roles as much as any other component of Sport Education

4. You must have some form of accountability so that student performance in these crucial roles counts for something toward team success.

5. You should provide the materials needed for the roles to be fulfilled appropriately.

Clearly Define Roles

It is important that you clearly define the roles you choose. Students need to know exactly what each role entails, which may involve some responsibility before, during, and after a game, and in some cases, beyond the class time. Many teachers will develop small booklets that explain the duties of each role and describe precisely the tasks that need to be accomplished and when they need to be done. Other teachers prepare posters that describe the duties for each role. At the very least you should develop a captain's notebook explaining all the responsibilities for the team captain. Teachers typically require that booklets be returned in good shape after the season. You can include this requirement in a team captain contract (see figure 3.1) or have teams receive points toward the seasonal championship by returning booklets in good condition. Teachers who have used Sport Education for several years typically create team booklets that contain information related to the key roles to be occupied by players on that team.

Many teachers choose to develop contracts as methods of clearly defining a role and its responsibilities. For example, in the team captain contract shown in figure 3.1, the captain will first read aloud the contract to his or her team, and will then sign the pledge. In addition, each member of that team will also sign, indicating their support for the captain and acknowledging their commitment to work with the captain in positive ways during the upcoming season.

The accompanying CD-ROM includes one-page sample **role cards** for the roles described. They can be used as part of the team booklets or team binders. The role cards include brief role descriptions, specific tasks and responsibilities, and the required knowledge and skills to be successful in the role. Separate role cards are provided for use at the elementary school and secondary school level. The elementary school level role cards have been split into beginner level (i.e., when implementing Sport Education for the first time) and experienced level.

**Student Roles/
Role Cards**

Allocate Time to Learning Roles

When designing the season plan, you need to allocate time in early season lessons for students to learn and practice their roles, especially the roles of referee and scorekeeper, roles which will be occupied by all students in the season. You should provide sample score sheets, statistics forms, and other forms and guides for fulfilling role responsibilities. You should clearly explain the significance of the role and communicate your expectation that each student's performance in that role should contribute to the success of the season.

Of particular importance are the lessons where students learn to officiate contests and keep score and statistics. During these lessons, some teachers invite officials from local associations to help students learn the finer points of positioning; others show videos of games to illustrate how the officials move about the field and how they give their signals. They take time to show the score sheet and statistics kept for each contest, help students to understand what each of the

Team Captain Contract

Team name:_____   Sport:_____

Grade:_____   Class/homeroom teacher:_____

As Team Captain, I will lead by example in showing good sporting behavior and leadership in the following areas:

- **Fair play**—I will play by the game rules and class rules.

- **Full effort**—I will work hard in all aspects of the class (practice, fitness, and games).

- **Respect**—I will show respect toward teammates, officials, opponents, teacher, and equipment.

- **Responsibility**—I will organize my players for practices and before all games.

- **Assistance**—I will get all my players to want to improve and I will assist them in improving.

Team captain's specific duties

- Take attendance.

- If necessary, call team meetings where concerns can be discussed.

- Submit team practice plan on a daily basis.

- Assist the teacher with line-ups for games.

- Act as a spokesperson for the team.

- Check for safe behavior by teammates and others.

- Return team booklet in good condition at end of season.

Team captain's signature:_____   Date:_____

Team members' signatures:

_____   _____

_____   _____

_____   _____

_____   _____

_____   _____

Figure 3.1   Sample team captain contract. You can also find this contract on the accompanying CD-ROM.

statistics mean (e.g., rebounds, assists, and steals in basketball), and practice filling out the score sheet. For example, you can show a 10-minute video of a game and all students will fill out the score and statistics sheet for what they saw. You can then assess student understanding of their responsibilities and provide feedback to correct scoring errors. A second task during this training phase is to reinforce the concept of how officials serve to enhance competition rather than take away from it. You should explain that student officials are beginners; they too are learning a new skill, and hence should be treated with the same respect as others in the class who are learning new sport techniques and tactics. This task is quite important to the fair play system described in chapter 7.

Help Students Practice Their Roles

Students need practice at performing these roles as much as in any other component of sport education. In the previous section we described how you can help students to learn the skills of refereeing and scorekeeping. You also have to plan opportunities for students to practice these skills in a gamelike context. You should plan practices to be early in the season so that when practice matches are scheduled early in the season, time is not spent in games that do not work. In helping students learn the roles involved in officiating a game (e.g., referee, scorekeeper, statistician, or judge), you may stop a practice game to check that the officials have made or recorded the appropriate response. In their very first refereeing role, many students may be hesitant to become assertive with their whistles, or they may be indecisive in making their calls. It is your role to intervene in these games, first to help the official learn the correct signals or decisions and then to support that official as the legitimate authority of the contest. Students will get better as they get more experience, know the activity better, and gain confidence in their role. Then you will spend less time focusing on the roles.

Intervention does not apply only to referees and line judges but also to statisticians and scorekeepers. For example, in a Frisbee game, a record will be made of the receiver and thrower of a touchdown. You can develop a protocol where the scorer and thrower inform the statistician of their names, or you may give this task to the referee. In the earliest lessons, you should stop play to teach or reinforce this protocol so that the more important games later in the season run smoothly. You also need to give the statistician the power to stop the game and clarify a point in cases where they are unsure of a decision. This is particularly helpful in the early stages of a season, where students are learning the scoring systems, and where interruptions to games are of less importance.

A WORD ON STATISTICS

Chapter Slides

First, do not make the statistics too complex, and do not have too many statistics or the students will struggle to keep up with the play. Rather, use the finite actions of the play as the statistics to be recorded. In invasion games, these statistics may include interceptions, goals or touchdowns, and in some cases assists. For batting and fielding games, simple statistics may include hits, runs, runs batted in, put outs, assists, and errors.

In determining which statistics are kept, it is important to understand the history of the sport, and to take note of the statistics in that sport's history that have the most meaning. Remember, you are teaching sport literacy as part of sport education and you want students to understand some of the benchmark scores.

Of course, in cases where the students have devised new games within their own classes or schools, they may be used to develop school histories of records. Like refereeing, scorekeeping will get easier as students gain experience in Sport Education. The skills necessary for scorekeeping not only carry over from a seventh grade volleyball season to an eighth grade volleyball season, but also from one sport to another, because the concepts associated with scorekeeping get practiced in multiple settings.

CREATING CONDITIONS FOR SUCCESSFUL PERFORMANCE

Successful Sport Education teachers use three key strategies to optimize the probability that students will perform well in their various roles: emphasizing the importance of roles, holding students accountable for role performance, and preparing materials necessary for role performance. If you do these three teacher tasks well, your students will not only enthusiastically perform well in their roles, they will also embrace the importance of those roles for team and season success.

Emphasize the Importance of Roles

In addition to explaining role performance requirements and providing opportunities for students to practice their roles, you need to consistently emphasize the importance of good role performance for the team and the entire class to enjoy the season. You can emphasize the importance of role performance in numerous ways: You can display posters in the gymnasium highlighting the importance of a referee or a team fitness specialist. Your materials describing role performance can also include brief descriptions of how important the role is and how performing well in the role contributes to team and class success. You can use verbal prompts during class to bring attention to the roles. By providing positive and corrective feedback to students you can signify the importance you attach to having them do well in their roles. Finally, by publicly recognizing good role performance during class and at class closure, you not only reinforce good role performance for the individual recognized but clearly demonstrate to students how valuable you consider such performances.

Assign Students Accountability for Role Performance

Students should understand that they will be held accountable for their role performance. You cannot expect students to apply themselves to a role unless it counts for team and individual assessment.

In terms of assessment, many teachers will provide space within the season scoring system for the accomplishment of a team's administrative duties. For example, during a floor hockey league, one teacher allocated points to each team following the completion of its performance as the duty team. The points were distributed as shown in table 3.4.

In this evaluation form, all duty team members were held responsible for actions before, during, and after the match. Many of the criteria relate to organization (e.g., getting games started on time and returning equipment and forms), while others focus more on the team's ability to perform its role in the course of a match. Both of these features of duty teams are important for running a season smoothly.

Table 3.4 Point Allocation During a Floor Hockey Season

Task	Complete	Incomplete
Equipment returned Whistle and puck returned (by the referee) Line judges shirts returned Score sheet returned Statistics sheet returned Pencils returned	1 point	0 points
Score sheet completed fully and accurately Both team names provided Final score indicated Fair play points clearly indicated	1 point	0 points
Statistics sheet completed fully and accurately Both team names provided Goal tallies match the official score sheet Goal scorers clearly indicated	1 point	0 points
Duty team evaluation (completed by the playing teams) Did the duty team arrive at the game on time and ready? Did the duty team get the game started on time? Did the duty team pay attention during the game?	1 point per "yes"	
Referee evaluation (completed by the playing teams) Did the referee know the rules? Did the referee conduct a fair contest? Was the referee paying attention during the game?	1 point per "yes"	

You can hold students individually accountable for their role performance. For example, you can include a student's performance at officiating or scoring within their course evaluation. Likewise, you may also award points for participation in optional activities such as membership on the sport governing board or activities as a publicist. Another important form of informal accountability is giving awards at the end of the season. You can include awards for successful completion of various roles at an end-of-season awards ceremony.

Prepare Materials

It is your responsibility to secure all the materials needed to make the season move forward smoothly. You can find many forms and materials needed to plan and implement a Sport Education season on the CD-ROM. These materials can include not only the equipment necessary for skills practices and for game play, but also schedules, coaches' instructions, lineup cards, results sheets, scorekeeping sheets, statistics sheets, cumulative statistics records, and awards. Remember, the evidence suggests that students become really involved with their season. You do not want to reduce their motivation by not having appropriate materials ready when they are needed.

Many teachers have had success in developing a coaches' notebook or **team binder.** This book may include some or all of the following items:

- List of coach's responsibilities
- Schedule of competition

Team Binder Template

- Game or match rules in effect for competitions
- Entry forms for various competitions
- Duties of referees and scorekeepers
- Forms for assigning referees and scorekeepers for competitions
- Skills and strategy information for the sport
- Specific safety concerns for coaches
- Point system for overall team competition

As with the captain's notebook and other booklets discussed earlier, teachers typically require that coach and team notebooks be returned in good shape at the close of the season and they award points toward the seasonal championship for doing so. They also often include the requirement in the coach's contract that is signed at the start of the season.

When students begin to play matches, you may prepare a duty team box that includes all the equipment necessary for conducting a game. This box will contain referees' jerseys, whistles, score and statistics sheets, pencils, evaluation forms, and even game balls. The duty team will be responsible for returning all the items of this box at the completion of competition. The team manager is typically responsible for seeing that this responsibility is completed successfully.

Chapter Slides

INCLUDING ALL STUDENTS

In typical physical education classes, many students with physical limitations find themselves as outsiders during sport units. In Sport Education, these students can make significant contributions to their teams. First, students with physical limitations can complete many of the important nonplaying roles, such as scorekeeper and statistician, no differently from other students. Second, these students can play important roles in team leadership, such as fitness leader, team manager, Sports Board representative, or sports reporter. While some physical conditions may not allow students to demonstrate all skills involved in a particular sport, they can still be considered as captains or coaches. Throughout history, teams have been led by inspiring players who themselves have not been the best players.

The same is true for students with low skill levels and students who typically do not participate. Research throughout the world has shown that these students tend to thrive in the Sport Education model because they become members of teams where they are supported by their teammates and what they do counts toward team success every bit as much as do the contributions of more-skilled students. These students should also have equal access to important roles on the team.

SPORTS BOARD AND DISPUTE RESOLUTION COMMITTEE

**Student Roles
Sports Board**

Many teachers choose to include a sport committee or **sports board** as a feature of their sport education seasons. This feature is particularly beneficial in middle and secondary schools because it provides a major role for students and creates a mechanism whereby students can make decisions and arbitrate disputes themselves, thus contributing to the curriculum's personal growth goals.

Members of the sports board advise teachers in concerns relating to the overall policies governing the sport education season, and they can make final decisions concerning fair play rules, competition schedules, and the like. Some of the duties of the sports board include planning the competitions with the teacher, dealing with disputes or student requests, meeting with the teacher to share ideas and feedback from students, providing positive role models for teams, planning the culminating event, and ensuring the smooth day-to-day functioning of the program.

If you decide to include a sports board in your curriculum, you should provide a clear explanation to students about their roles and responsibilities. In particular, you should remind students that sports board membership involves a willingness to spend time in meetings and discussions outside of regular class time.

> **W**hen the teachers just give you the rules, many people do not take much notice of them. Then, when you get in a game, everyone has their own idea of what should be happening, and they all fuss and argue. It ends up with someone getting mad and causing a fight. In this season, where the board made up the rules of play and we all voted on them, since everyone knew and agreed on what was going on, and how they all knew exactly what to do, there didn't end up being any fussing.
>
> —Seventh grade student, USA

While you may prefer not to involve the complete sports board concept, you may wish to use students in the role of **dispute resolution.** This group can meet when required to make decisions concerning violations of fair play rules or respond to complaints from officials. An extract from interviews with ninth grade students shows how effective this committee can be:

3

Student Roles/ Dispute Resolution Committee

> "So far we've only had like one complaint that we had to deal with and that was only swearing so we just made that person have a suspension for two games." "I don't think she wants to swear again because otherwise she will let her team down, but she didn't mind being taken off because she knew she swore." "The little shock we've given her will make sure that she won't do that in the future because she knows the consequences now." (Carlson & Hastie, JTPE, 1997, p. 185)

Physical educators have always proclaimed that their subject matter influences personal and social development. In many instances, however, little has been done to specifically address goals of personal and social development that are potentially embedded within the subject matter. Sport Education takes these goals seriously. The feature of multiple roles is a key part of the model that contributes to these important goals. Roles need to be defined, taught, and practiced. Students need to be held accountable for performing well in the roles, both through formal means in a seasonal point system and through informal means through teacher feedback and recognition for improved performance. If teachers take the student roles feature of Sport Education seriously, the students will too.

Personal and social development does not happen in isolation. It always happens within an important social context, which in Sport Education is the team. Heterogeneous teams require that students help and support one another if they are to be successful as a team. Each team member has a contribution to make, and it is in the best interests of the team for members to help and support each other. Each team member has responsibilities. When they acquit themselves well in their various roles, their contributions are valued by teammates. We are not foolish enough to believe that all this happens automatically; we know it takes work. It takes good planning and support from the teacher. But, evidence shows that it can and does happen!

It's been a great experience. . . . It developed my skills as a coach and I enjoyed being part of the team as well.

—Tenth grade student, New Zealand

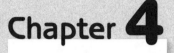

Chapter 4

Selecting Teams and Coaches

Sport Education students become members of teams early in the season and maintain their affiliation with that team throughout the season. The idea of teams is fundamental to the Sport Education model because it forms the basis for the pedagogical approach that makes Sport Education successful: persisting, small learning groups. In typical PE programs, teams are formed only for the duration of a contest. In SE settings, students not only play together as a team, but practice skills, develop tactics, and complete administrative tasks as a team for the entire season. The persisting membership on a team, the performances of individuals that contribute to a team performance, and the many duties that teams must carry out for the season to be successful, together create situations in which responsibility and personal growth can take place.

Chapter Slides

> *I think we learned more having one of us being the coach because teachers can only teach you so much. They've got to get around to all the groups and they can't come over to you individually and spend a lesson just with you.*
>
> —Ninth grade student, Australia

Players and performers always have more fun and more of a challenge when the outcome of a contest or event is uncertain. That is why games are better when the competitors and teams are evenly matched. No one, especially the players, enjoys a very uneven contest. For games and contests to be even, the competitors must be as evenly matched as possible. In Sport Education you must make every effort to select evenly matched teams so that each team has a chance to be successful. With this objective achieved, the outcome of the competition will depend more on the ability of the students to work together to solve tactical and interpersonal problems than would be the case if teams were uneven. Placing students on evenly matched teams depends very much on what sport you choose. For example, teams that would be even for soccer might not be even for gymnastics. In this chapter we will describe concerns related to making decisions about the number of teams within a class. We will then provide multiple proven methods for selecting teams and coaches and for assigning coaches to teams.

TEAM SIZE AND NUMBER OF TEAMS

Before deciding how to form student teams, you must determine how many teams to have for that season. Team size is determined by a number of factors, including

- how the activity is modified,
- what kinds of competitions are planned for that modified activity (see chapter 5),
- how easily absences can be handled, and
- how students can manage the daily tasks of practice and competition.

Most Sport Education teachers choose to embed small-sided teams into larger teams. For example, in elementary soccer, teachers have had great success dividing classes into three teams of 8 to 10 students each. This type of season might have three competitions, allowing students to learn skills and tactics in competitions that were very simple to start with and then more complex as team size increased. If the season started with a 2v2 competition, each team would field three to five teams. If this competition were followed by a 3v3 competition, the team could field two to three teams. (The number chosen would depend on predictable absences.) A season final competition of 6v6 would see each team field one team and use substitutions so that all students would get equal playing time. The smaller-sided competitions would allow less-skilled students to compete against each other and more-skilled students to do so also, with each outcome counting equally toward the seasonal championship. Choosing coed teams also allows for a format where you can have a boy's competition, a girl's competition, and a coed competition. This format appears to be the easiest method to cover for absences and still move the season forward smoothly.

A major benefit of creating an odd number of teams is that it allows for full utilization of what is called the duty team. For example, using the soccer model just described, if the first competition on a particular day involved two-person teams representing team 1 and team 2, then team 3 would be the duty team. It would provide all the referees and scorekeepers for those games and would also be responsible for seeing that teams were in the right spot to begin the game and that equipment was where it should be. After the 2v2 games pitting team 1 versus team 2 was over, then the next games might pit team 1 versus team 3 with the students from team 2 performing all the duty chores.

If you plan just a single competition (e.g., 3v3 volleyball) with some preseason scrimmages and then a series of games, the team size model noted previously also appears to be the best solution. Each larger team could have two or three smaller teams, with team assignment determined by skill levels. Absences would be less problematic, and the duty team would provide all the management, refereeing, and scorekeeping when not competing. Much can be said for small-sided teams that play against teams of relatively equal skill levels. It is more fun for the players, and they tend to get more opportunities to learn skills and strategies. And, each of them contributes equally to overall team success.

14 Chapter Slides

SELECTING STUDENTS TO TEAMS

Few subjects will engender more student concern than the method of team selection. The following suggestions about team selection have been compiled from teacher feedback and comments based on their experiences using Sport Education. Remember, no matter what decisions you make in this area, students will have concerns. Our experiences in Sport Education tell us that students are extremely concerned about fairness. They want fair teams and equal competition. Team selection interests them greatly, providing key opportunities to teach and reinforce the concept of fairness.

You may choose to be totally responsible for team selection, or you may work in conjunction with students. Many Sport Education teachers who work at the elementary level do most of the team selection themselves. Others do the selection themselves until students get experience in the Sport Education model and then they begin to bring students into the selection process. At the high school level, especially in Australia and New Zealand, students select teams, often by creating another important Sport Education role, that of team selector. Which selection method you use will depend on the answers to the following questions:

- How well do you know your students?
- How well do the students know each other?
- How familiar are the students with the sport you have chosen?
- How familiar are the students with the Sport Education model?

Because one purpose of sport education is to encourage students to gradually assume more responsibility for directing and managing their own sport experiences, you might consider gradually bringing students into the selection process. When you choose to involve students in team selection, you have two options: you may work with team coaches, or you may have a selection panel. When using student coaches, you must first determine how to choose the coaches. The most common methods for **selecting coaches** are as follows:

Selecting Team Coaches

- The teacher assigns coaches at the beginning of the season.
- Students apply to be coaches, using written nomination forms describing their skills, talents, and leadership qualities (see figure 4.1).
- Students vote by secret ballot on who they wish to have as coaches.

You can use a similar process when a student panel assists you in team selection. Students may volunteer, apply, or be voted onto this panel, according to criteria determined by you. In the case of a selection panel, the panel should have some knowledge of the skills and abilities of the students in the class and of the activity that will be the focus of the season.

Once you have decided whether or not to use students in team selection, numerous formats are available for selecting teams. These formats do not include the familiar scenario of the public (and often humiliating) process where the most skillful in the class first select their friends, then those with average skills, and finally those with least skill. Table 4.1 lists various methods for placing students on teams. Some of these methods involve only the teacher, and can be done even before the season begins. Other methods may be more appropriate once you and your students have completed a season or two of Sport Education. In all cases, however, it is important to have students in teams as soon as possible, because a large part of the personal growth resulting from good sport experiences is intimately related to students having a team affiliation in which their actions impact the team's success.

Team Coach Application Form

Name:_____ Date:_____ Class period:_____

Sport:_____ Team:_____

I would be an effective team coach because:

I have the following leadership qualities:

I have the following skills needed to be a good team coach:

Use the back of this form for more writing space

Signature:_____

Figure 4.1 Sample team coach application form.

Table 4.1 Methods for Selecting Teams

Selection method	Teacher	Selection panel	Coaches
Allocation of students to even teams	X	X	
Performance scores	X	X	X
Skills challenges	X	X	X
Tournament rankings	X	X	
3-2-1 rating system		X	X
Draft system			X
Blind draft			X

Preseason Allocation of Students to Teams by the Teacher

Who: Teacher independent of students
When: Before the season begins

In this option, which normally occurs when teachers know their students well, the teacher selects teams before the season commences. During the first lesson, the teacher announces the teams, assigns teams their home spaces, and in many cases asks students to choose a team name and team color. Even teams refer not only to evenness in terms of skill but also to balance of gender, ethnicity, and personality. That is not to say that you should change team members at the first sign of a personality conflict. Part of the process of Sport Education is students learning to come together, to experience the ups and downs of an extended season, and to learn to maximize the skills and talents of all team members for the benefit of their teams.

> *T*he first day I announced teams, these five students sat in three separate piles and pouted. They would not even look at each other, let alone discuss a team name. We told them to just deal with it. Well, by the end of season, this team was in the Super Bowl, they played rotating quarterbacks, and had just about the best level of team harmony and spirit I've seen from 5th graders.
>
> —Elementary school teacher, USA

Preseason Allocation of Students to Teams by the Teacher and Students

Who: Teacher and student coaches or selection panel
When: Before the season begins

An extension of the first option is for the teacher to involve students in the selecting even teams. These students often offer valuable insight into the potential of varying students, particularly in terms of getting along with others. Using students to select teams also empowers them to take responsibility in their class. Student selectors can be appointed by the teacher or elected by their classmates, using a secret ballot. Like most roles in Sport Education, if this form of selection is chosen, then all students should eventually learn the role of selector. The accompanying **CD-ROM offers several checklists** and rating scales to aid you and student selectors in assessing the incoming technical and game performance level of students as part of the team selection process. If you are comfortable using a PDA, you will find the electronic versions useful for collecting and compiling player information. Otherwise, print versions are also provided.

Player Assessment

Performance Scores

Who: Teacher and student coaches or selection panel
When: As early as possible

In this format, scores from particular tests may be used to allocate students to even teams. For example, during the early lessons of an aerobic dance season students may perform a 1-mile run or an agility course run. You can use the times from these runs to place students on various teams. You can either use these data independently, or may involve a sports board or volunteer selectors in assigning students to teams in ways similar to those described earlier.

Skill Challenges

Who: Teacher and student coaches or selection panel
When: Following initial skill instruction lessons

Similar to the previous method, you may conduct a number of skills challenges or tests to gather information for placing students on teams. For example, in the early lessons of a volleyball season, students will rotate through three stations where they complete the tasks of serving, overhead passing, and continuous volleying. You or the selection committee will then use the scores from these stations to place students on even teams.

Small Tournaments

Who: Teacher and student coaches or selection panel
When: Following a mini-tournament early in the season

In one example from a New Zealand tennis season, students participated in a singles tournament early in the season. The results from this tournament were used to rank students and create teams for the remainder of the season. Any of the racket sports would suit this format, although one-on-one games can be created for many sports such as soccer or basketball.

Student Selection Committee Using a Rating Scale

Who: Student coaches or selection panel
When: Before the season begins

In this method, students work independently to create even teams. What is often helpful in this process is to have the students first rank all students in the class on a 3-2-1 scale, from expert to beginner. From here, the level 3 players (considered to be on the expert level) can be allocated evenly across teams, followed by level 2 players and then level 1 players (considered to be on the beginner level). One way of testing the evenness of teams is to check whether the total score for each team is the same as all others. After this evenness is achieved, players of equal ranking can be shuffled from one team to another to balance gender and ethnicity, and to avoid internal team disharmony. Once teams are formed, they are then announced by the committee or are posted on the physical education notice board.

Draft System

Who: Student coaches
When: During the first two or three lessons

In a draft system, all players perform a series of skills for the coaches. As the students perform their skills, the coaches take notes and then conduct a conference in which they select teams. For example, in one softball season, each player completed a tryout. The five coaches scouted the talent and used a draft card to tabulate the data on each student. The tryout skills included a 60-yard dash for time, fielding ground balls, fielding fly balls, throwing to a base, and hitting. The teacher met with the coaches at the completion of the tryout day, and then set up a time to meet to conduct the draft. The draft was conducted privately and not during class time. Each resulting team consisted of eight players. The order of drafting switched with each round so that no team got an advantage. As shown in figure 4.2, the Black Hawks in this draft start with the second pick in the first round. In subsequent rounds, the order is rotated.

Teams		Randomly selected draft order		First round	Second round	Third round	Fourth round	Fifth round
Bruins		Braves		Braves	*Black Hawks*	Beavers	Bears	Bruins
Braves		*Black Hawks*		*Black Hawks*	Beavers	Bears	Bruins	Braves
Black Hawks		Beavers		Beavers	Bears	Bruins	Braves	*Black Hawks*
Beavers		Bears		Bears	Bruins	Braves	*Black Hawks*	Beavers
Bears		Bruins		Bruins	Braves	*Black Hawks*	Beavers	Bears

Figure 4.2 Sample draft selection order template.

Coaches Conduct a Blind Draft

Who: Student coaches
When: Before the season begins

A very useful method of using student-only selections is to have elected team coaches who then select teams in a private meeting. However, the coaches do not know which of those teams they will ultimately be on. It is only when they have completed team final selections that the coaches themselves are assigned to teams through a lottery. This method prevents a situation in which coaches may attempt to load up one particular team for their own benefit, because in the end they may not even be on that team.

Using Students As Selectors

No matter which selection format you choose, you should consider a number of factors. First, *all* students need to be considered as selectors, not just the most skilled students. However, when students are selecting teams independently of you, they should have some understanding of the sport itself. Second, you need to establish clear criteria for team selection. Ask students to consider the skill and fitness requirements of the game, to balance the number of boys and girls on each team, and to consider the leadership abilities of the members of each team, as well as the possibility of personality conflicts. Finally, it is important that all panel discussions remain confidential. When student teams are announced in class or posted on a notice board, give special attention to listing student names in alphabetical order rather than by the order in which they were selected. The accompanying CD-ROM includes two one-page charts that can be used to assist students in **selecting teams** and roles within each team.

TEAM AFFILIATION

Many students develop strong affiliation with their teams, an action you should promote in many ways, such as with team names, colors, cheers, and mascots. When promoting team affiliation, you will need to use set criteria that take into account cost and local standards, such as clothing restrictions. For example, team uniforms are a good idea, but may not be affordable. Picking a color scheme or adding a name or symbol to an article of clothing might be a more realistic alternative. Another inexpensive way to promote team affiliation is to place team photos on bulletin boards or with competition schedules. You can also organize gymnasium notice boards by team to reinforce the team concept. If you have the appropriate facilities, you can even have teams create their own Web sites.

Teams should have a home practice area in the gymnasium or playing field. Team members can report to this area at the start of class and do warm-ups and their own technique and strategy practice. Home team areas also provide you with a convenient time-saving routine for organizing students. For example, you can have coaches take attendance in home areas then report to you.

You can encourage teams to practice in nonattached time. Elementary teachers have used recess times as well as before and after school times for team practices. At higher grades, you can encourage teams to practice on their own in nonattached time. Ways of including out-of-class practice in assessment and accountability systems are described throughout the text. You can also encourage whole teams to enter school intramural competitions or local recreational competitions.

TEAM PORTFOLIOS

Another way in which some teachers have emphasized team affiliation has been through developing **team portfolios.** These portfolios allow students to demonstrate both individual and team strengths and weaknesses and serve to summarize their growth across each season. During the course of the season, teachers can allocate time at the end of specific lessons for team members to meet and discuss progress on their portfolios.

Portfolios usually have a cover page that includes the team's name, drawn logo, and shirt design. Further sections include the players' names (complete with player profiles), a team philosophy, and diary entries completed by different team members. For some seasons, teams can diagram their offensive and defensive plays. Of course, all teams are welcome to include portfolio items in addition to those on the required list of artifacts. In that way, students can organize their sport experiences, take control over the layout and content of their team portfolios, and decide on their own what kinds of learning they wish to demonstrate (Kinchin, 2001).

When using portfolios, teachers usually have each team designate its portfolio manager. This student is responsible for delegating individual responsibilities to team members to complete the portfolio, for bringing the portfolio to class (or collecting it from the teacher) so final artifacts can be included, for talking to the teacher about any problems with the completion of the portfolio, and for submitting the final file when it is due.

Selecting team membership and assigning coaches to teams is an important step in building a successful Sport Education season. Once students become accustomed to the Sport Education model, this aspect of teacher planning will become much easier. Experience throughout the world has shown that students who gain experience in Sport Education become very concerned about fairness in student assignment to teams. Experience has also shown that many different types of students can function effectively as coaches. Eventually, over the course of many seasons, one would expect that each student would have the opportunity to fill the role of coach.

Chapter 5

Creating Modified Games

14

Chapter Slides

A key feature of Sport Education is that it provides developmentally appropriate games for children and youth. In chapter 1, we introduced the idea of modified games. Throughout this chapter, we use the term games in its broadest sense, to include sports as well as activities used in Sport Education. In the development of KiwiSport, a national program of sport for children and youth, the Hillary Commission of New Zealand refers to a modified game as one that resembles the sport on which it is based, and has been adapted to suit the players' age, size, ability, health status, skill level, and experience.

The fundamental nature of a game is defined by the basic problem that needs to be solved (Almond, 1986; Siedentop, 2004). For example, the basic problem to solve in volleyball is to strike the ball over a net in a divided court in such a way that it either cannot be returned by opponents or hits the floor within bounds. The primary rule (or rules) of the game defines the way in which the problem is to be solved. Changing a primary rule simply changes the game. For example, the primary rule in volleyball is that the ball must be struck; that is, volleyball is a striking game, not a passing and catching game. Secondary rules such as the number of hits, the height of the net, the size of the court, and the type of the ball can be modified without changing the basic nature of the game. In fact, they should be changed to help students improve their techniques and tactics so they can eventually play what is typically called the parent game. The primary rule in soccer is the handball rule, which disallows striking the ball with the hands. Secondary rules should be altered so that fields are smaller, the ball is friendlier, the numbers of players on each side allow for all learners to be frequently involved in the action at the ball, and off-the-ball tactics are less complex.

A modified game does not lessen the challenge of play, but rather matches an appropriate level of challenge to the developmental status of the learners. Modified games also provide players with opportunities to practice techniques and tactics in situations that match their current level of learning and their abilities, and to do so in ways that allow them to progress toward the parent game. Modifications can include alterations to secondary rules such as size, weight or style of equipment, playing area, length of the game, rules, number of players in teams, size of goals, heights of nets, the rotation of player positions, or methods of scoring. The fundamental basis of modifying games is to put the needs of young people first.

Chapter Slides

KEY STRATEGIES FOR MODIFYING GAMES

The following key strategies for modifying games will keep games fun and challenging, and allow students to be successful. The nature of the modifications will always be situation specific, depending on your knowledge of your students' abilities. These strategies are (a) make scoring easier, (b) slow the movement of the ball or object, (c) increase opportunities to practice techniques and tactics, (d) sequence games to enable the learning of tactics, and (e) change the scoring rules.

Make Scoring Easier

When playing in a game or contest, youngsters like to score. Scoring is an important way (but not the only way) to define success. Scoring also reinforces the use of appropriate techniques and tactics. When scoring is infrequent, children tend to get frustrated. For example, when children are taught to play basketball with a 10-foot hoop and a regulation ball in a five-a-side format, scoring is infrequent with inappropriate techniques and tactics often unwittingly fostered. We have watched many middle school PE volleyball games with a regulation net and ball, in which 80% of the points scored are from unreturned serves because students have no mastery over the important skill of passing. The essence of volleyball is the rally, with most scoring occurring with hits at or near the net. The most direct way to accomplish this kind of rally is to eliminate the serve and start each rally with what is called a free ball.

You can increase the likelihood of scoring in many ways. For example, using lower basketball goals, larger soccer goals, and shorter rackets with larger heads (that allow for more control) all tend to increase the appropriate use of techniques and tactics for scoring. Friendly pitchers in softball increase the pace of play and the number of hits. Balls that are softer, larger, and that move through the air more slowly also tend to increase scoring through more appropriate use of offensive techniques and strategies.

Slow the Movement of the Ball or Object

It is difficult for beginners to execute techniques appropriately if they are not in position to do so. In developing games sense (see chapter 2), youngsters gradually learn how to anticipate the movement of objects, teammates, and opponents, thus allowing them to move to advantageous positions enabling them to make the next play, which keeps the flow of the game moving forward. Slowing the movement of the ball or object is particularly important in court-divided games such as volleyball, badminton, and tennis. It is of great help if the object moves more slowly while students acquire the capacity to anticipate and move to appropriate positions. This same approach is also appropriate for invasion games (soccer, lacrosse, floor hockey, and so on) in which the regulation ball often moves so quickly that beginners cannot get in position to successfully continue the flow of play. You can accomplish this goal in a number of ways, but the two most important are using a friendlier, slower object and increasing the height of the net dividing the court.

You can either purchase or make balls and objects that move through space and along the ground or floor more slowly than regulation balls or objects. In volleyball, teachers of younger children might start with balloons, then move to balloons covered with cloth, then to a volley-trainer ball which is 25 percent larger and 40 percent lighter than regulation, then to a soft-touch regulation ball. Many manufacturers now produce balls and other equipment that is more friendly for learning techniques and tactics (see table 5.1). Moving the net higher automatically slows down the pace of the game because the ball or object has to be hit on a higher trajectory to get it over the net. This modification allows players to move into position to execute the appropriate technique and keep the flow of the game moving.

Table 5.1 Enabling Learning With Modified Equipment

Equipment	Description/benefit
No-sting Ragball volleyball	Ball gives on impact, reduces fear, slows game
VB-Trainer	40% lighter, 25% larger, slows game
VB-Trainer II	25% lighter, regulation size, slows game
Regulation ball	Sequence of balls for volleyball
Softey Ball	Official size and weight softball but limited flight, reduces fear
Ragballs	9" baseballs, 11" softballs, 16" softballs Softer, safer, slower flight, reduces flight, reduces fear
Maxi Net-n-Goal System	Can be organized for 2 volleyball nets at 3 different heights, 3 badminton nets, 3 short-court tennis or racquetball nets, or 2 basketball goals at 4 different heights.
Mix-and-match head/shafts	Plastic shafts at 5 different lengths to which different heads can be attached for lacrosse and floor hockey.
Hang-a-Hoops	Basketball hoops that can be hung at any height and in regulation and large sizes.

All of these products are available from Sportime (www.sportime.com).

A third strategy, effective in the very early stages of learning the court and net game of volleyball, is to allow students to catch the ball instead of using techniques such as sets and forearm passes. It offers increased chances of students being successful and develops more flow in the game. Especially in small-sided (e.g., 2v2 and 3v3) games, it creates a game situation where, offensively, students learn about effective ball placement (e.g., deep in the opponents' court or in uncovered areas); while defensively, students can learn more quickly the importance of defensive court coverage (e.g., base position) and making adjustments. In traditional approaches to teaching volleyball (those with a technical orientation), students tend to not recognize the importance of moving to the ball. Being allowed to catch and then redirect a ball is another way of slowing down the game, offering a bit more time to make a decision about where or to whom to direct the ball, and thus creating more chances for success. How long you allow students to make use of catching the ball depends on how well players are developing their ability to control the ball and anticipate the game's action.

5
Sample Modified Games

Increase Opportunities to Practice Techniques and Tactics

Sample Modified Games

The most important strategy for achieving this goal is to reduce team size. Sport Education teachers hardly ever use regulation-sized teams. Most experts who study the conditions under which techniques and tactics are learned would agree that successful repetitions in a gamelike context is the key to improvement and eventually to students becoming skilled games players. In 11v11 soccer and 6v6 volleyball, students simply get too few opportunities to respond (OTRs) during the course of a game. It should be no surprise that 2v2 beach volleyball and 3v3 outdoor summer basketball competitions have become so popular. They allow for more action for each player than is possible in the parent game.

In games such as basketball, volleyball, and even soccer, most of what students need to learn in terms of tactics can be learned in a 3v3 format. In such a format, students get more touches and more opportunities to score, helping them to learn tactics and techniques more quickly. The reduced complexity of small-sided games also helps them to more quickly grasp the tactical nature of the games.

Striking and fielding games such as softball and cricket are notorious for their lack of involvement by many players. In a PE class softball game, it would not be unusual for a number of players, even though they are in the game, to not touch the ball for an entire class period, and they might get just one chance to bat. Softball and cricket are sector games that can be modified to make them fun and useful for small-sided teams. Softball, for example, is played on a 90-degree sector, while cricket is played on a 360-degree sector. Figure 5.1 shows how a smaller sector (35 to 40 degrees) can be arranged for a modified form of softball in which students get frequent opportunities to hit and field. Figure 5.2 shows how a series of small-sector softball games can be arranged to allow 30 to 40 students to be actively involved in play and get many OTRs for batting, fielding, and throwing. Use of a friendly pitcher (either from the batting team or the duty team) makes these games move even more quickly.

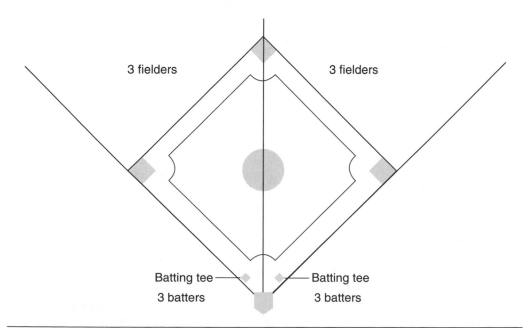

Figure 5.1 Dividing a regulation field for small-sector games.

Reprinted, by permission, from A. Launder, 2001, *Play practice* (Champaign, IL: Human Kinetics), 134.

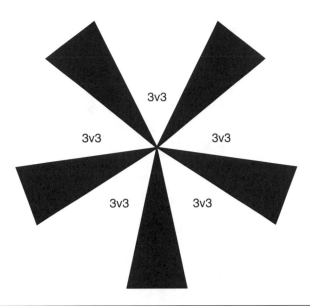

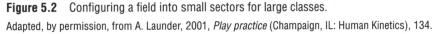

Figure 5.2   Configuring a field into small sectors for large classes.

Adapted, by permission, from A. Launder, 2001, *Play practice* (Champaign, IL: Human Kinetics), 134.

A final suggestion for helping students more easily learn techniques and tactics is to use a friendly guarding rule in both court and field invasion games. When students are beginning to learn a sport and are closely guarded by defenders, they tend either to panic and try immediately to get rid of the ball or they try to dribble or run away from the defender. A rule of friendly guarding simply means that defenders must be one arm's length away from the player they are guarding. This spacing enables the offensive player to try to execute techniques and to move more easily in a manner that is tactically appropriate. Students who guard more closely than an arm's length are simply called for a foul, with play resuming as quickly as possible. Friendly guarding is also a useful strategy for students to learn appropriate defensive positioning relative to the person being guarded, the flow of play, and the goal being guarded.

Sequence Games to Enable the Learning of Tactics

Invasion games present the most complex and difficult tactics for students to master. Court-divided games, such as volleyball or tennis, tend to be more predictable in their tactical demands and thus less difficult to master. Many girls and boys who learn invasion games and are thrust into large teams using large spaces, simply get bewildered, confused, and discouraged. It is no wonder that many youngsters quickly come to dislike invasion games. Some students are clever enough that they learn to be part of the flow of the game but to stay away from the main action, often successfully hiding their lack of participation. We call these students competent bystanders (Tousignant & Siedentop, 1983).

The easiest way to break down the tactics of invasion games and help students gradually to become more comfortable with increasingly more complex tactics is to use a series of small-sided games. Bell and Darnell (1994) described a series of soccer competitions for elementary school children that illustrate this principle: First, a 1v1 competition was played in a manner similar to half-court basketball. To play 1v1 games successfully, students must be able to dribble, shield, and shoot while on offense, and maintain defensive space and tackle on defense. In brief timed games (3 to 5 minutes) students get many opportunities to respond. Even inside the space of an elementary school gymnasium it is possible to have 8 such games going on simultaneously. Next was a 2v2 competition played as a full court game by simply combining two of the 1v1 spaces. In this game the concepts of tandem defending were introduced and offensive players learned passing, trapping, cutting, and floor balance. This game was followed by a 3v3 competition in which goalie, defender, and forward positions (or two forwards and a goalie) were used. In the 3v3 game, throw-ins, goal kicks, and corner kicks were introduced. In 3v3, the tactical concepts of players maintaining floor balance, cutting to positions of advantage, and centering the ball become important. Off-the-ball play becomes more obvious, both for defenders and attackers. You can use similar strategies for court invasion games such as basketball and floor hockey.

The size and configuration of the game space also helps to determine how tactics are learned. In field invasion games especially, the space should be large relative to the number of players to allow for more time for players to adjust to the movement of the ball, teammates, and opponents. As students progress in their game sense, you can make the space smaller so that it becomes even more important for players to value space and apply attacking or defending tactics. Altering spaces can also make some tactics more appropriate than others. For example, a longer, narrower space tends to produce longer passes, shots, or hits.

Change the Scoring Rules

You can also modify games by changing the scoring rules. Because the object of the game is to outscore the opponent, you can use this motivation to emphasize utilizing some techniques and tactics rather than others. We call this technique differential scoring. You can modify the typical point rules to give more points for what you want students to focus on. You can also modify the point system by adding negative points; that is, taking away points from the team's total for play that you want to discourage. In volleyball, awarding 2 points rather than 1 point for a team that scores through a pass-set-spike pattern encourages students to use the pass-set-spike pattern. In basketball, taking away a point for a basket scored by a player on a fast break without a teammate touching the ball will tend to eliminate the domination of the game by the more-skilled players.

14
Chapter Slides

MODIFYING INDIVIDUAL SPORTS

Most of the modifications that we make to individual sports relate to changes in equipment or modifications of the playing area. For example, using a weighted rod rather than an actual discus, and allowing throwers to release from behind a line rather than limiting them to a restrictive discus circle. Both these modifications allow for more positive and hence motivating experiences while still reinforcing the key biomechanical features of throwing a weight (e.g., hip rotation and the importance of keeping the hands back). The following sections give examples of how you can modify many individual sports to allow for more appropriate competition.

Track and Field Modifications
- Long jump or triple jump
  - Use an expanded takeoff board rather than the familiar narrow board.

- Have students run up and jump and measure from where their plant foot touched the takeoff board (or ground within an identified takeoff space).
- Discus
    - Use a weighted rod rather than the disc.
    - Use a front line rather than a circle.
- Shot put
    - Use a line rather than a circle.
    - Use lighter round objects, such as playground balls filled with water.
    - Do away with the foul line, and allow the throwers to propel themselves over the starting line.
- Javelin
    - Throw a blunted implement (plastic PVC pipe works well) and count distance by sector it lands in.
- Hurdles
    - Use lower hurdles.
    - Modify the distance between hurdles so that students learn the appropriate step sequence (e.g., 3 steps or 5 steps) between hurdles.
    - Reduce the number of hurdles in the race.

Swimming Modifications

- Allow the use of fins for those with less skill.
- Begin some races with swimmers already in the water.

Diving Modifications

- Include a category which has feet-first entries.
- Include fun categories such as "biggest splash."

Cross Country Running and Cross-Country Skiing Modifications

- Have different-length courses for varying fitness levels.
- Include varying obstacles for varying fitness levels.

Gymnastics Modifications

- Beam
    - Use a lower and wider bench rather than the narrow and high beam.
- Vault
    - Use a lower vaulting horse.
    - Increase the number of springs under the springboard.
    - Use a minitrampoline rather than a springboard.
- Floor exercises
    - Allow the use of cheese slice mats (a mat with a sloped surface) for assisting with rolls.
    - Incorporate larger mats or benches to assist in rotational movements.

MODIFYING DUAL SPORTS

As in individual sports, you can make significant modifications to the form of dual sports using changes in equipment. Using slower balls in tennis and pickleball make play more continuous and hence potentially more motivating, and allowing players to begin closer to targets can lead to more success and hence more enthusiasm. The following sections provide illustrations of how you can modify many dual sports to allow for more appropriate competition.

Racket Sports Modifications

- Tennis
    - Use a special slow tennis ball.
    - Use a racquetball racket or a tennis racket with a shorter handle.
    - Move the serve line in from the baseline.
- Pickleball
    - Use a slower, spongy ball rather than the regular plastic Wiffle ball.
    - Raise the net height.
    - Lengthen the baseline (allows for a lesser requirement to control power).
- Badminton
    - Use slower birdies.
    - Allow players to use the wider court for singles to emphasize angles (e.g., using cross-court shots).
    - Use a narrower, longer court to emphasize up-and-back play as students learn to master the clear and drop shots crucial to good badminton performance.

Target Sports Modifications

- Archery
    - Use larger overall targets, or targets with larger scoring rings.
    - Reduce the distance from the shooters to the target.
- Ten-pin bowling
    - Allow students to release the bowling ball closer to the pins.
    - Allow the use of bumpers (in the case of having access to actual bowling alleys).

MODIFYING TEAM SPORTS

Many team sports fit into the category of invasion games, those games in which a team has to gain possession of an object, move toward a specific target (progression), and score into that target. Basketball, soccer, water polo, lacrosse, and floor hockey are examples of these game forms.

To make these games more appropriate for students, you should first make modifications by reducing the number of players on each team. You should reduce the size of the playing area corresponding to the number of players. You should also reduce the number of rules and alter secondary rules to keep the game flowing (e.g., restart rules in soccer, pitching rules in softball). Following

Table 5.2   Modifications to Invasion Games

Equipment	Gaining possession	Progression	Scoring
Use larger balls. Use slower balls. Use shorter handles on striking implements (e.g., hockey sticks).	Do not allow one player to directly steal a ball from another player. Increase the ways in which a player can actually gain possession.	Allow players some steps in games where none is allowed (e.g., Frisbee). Increase the time an individual player can have possession without being penalized or in which he or she must make a pass. Reduce the pressure on a player as she or he attempts to put the ball in play after an out-of-bounds play or a penalty (e.g., do not allow players to stand too close to the sideline).	Make a goal larger. Make a goal lower. Consider including the opportunity of scoring by progressing the ball (or object) across an end line rather than into a specific goal.

these dimensional changes, you can make alterations at those levels previously mentioned (see table 5.2).

Other team sports fall into the category of batting and fielding games (also called sector games), of which softball and cricket are two examples. In these games, the key tactical areas relate to batting, fielding, player positioning, and base running, all of which are modifiable (see table 5.3).

In some games, students can learn tactics when taught the principles of attacking and defending. Principles such as maintaining spacing, creating angles, and running to open spaces can help students learn attacking tactics in soccer. Invasion games such as soccer and the hockey codes certainly use offensive and defensive tactics that, while based on the principles just cited, also create more predictable movement in reaction to offensive opportunities. In invasion games, such as basketball, the patterns become even more specific with player movement more predictable, both on offense and defense. In basketball teams should learn a patterned offense and either a person-to-person or zone defense. The attacking pattern should be as simple as possible, but one that can be learned and practiced. In 3v3 basketball, you might teach a simple attacking pattern that relies on a pass and screen away principle for use against person-to-person defenses. Students first learn the techniques of passing and catching. They also learn the important tactic of maintaining floor balance by moving to open spaces and creating triangles. They then follow the main principle of the offense; that is, they pass to one

Table 5.3   Modifications to Batting and Fielding Games

Equipment	Batting	Fielding	Base running
Use larger balls. Use shorter-handled bats.	Hit from a tee rather than a pitch. Allow the batter to receive a pitch or bowl from his or her own team. Have the duty team to provide a pitcher, aiming to present the batter friendly deliveries.	Have larger targets to hit (e.g., cricket). Reduce the size of the sector.	Limit the stealing options.

teammate and move away to screen for the other teammate, who cuts off that screen. The techniques needed for learning this offense are passing, catching, screening, reverse pivoting (for the screener who then can become another target for the passer), and backdoor cutting (if the defense overplays the open player on the attacking side). Students will then learn to become aware of how defenders play against this offensive tactic. For example, do defenders switch at the screen or try to stay with their primary defensive assignment? While the development and refinement of technique always takes a substantial amount of repetitive practice, students can learn tactics quickly once they grasp the significance and flow of the movements defined by the tactical scheme.

Chapter Slides

MODIFYING GAMES WITHIN CLASS

In upper elementary, middle, and high school classes, you can often expect to have students who have vastly different experiences in many sports; that is, most teachers expect heterogeneity of experience. Even when a season is designed around a sport that most students may have never seen yet alone played, you can expect substantial differences among students because of the carry-over from sports that require similar techniques and tactics. For example, team handball is a sport many American students would have never seen, let alone played. This invasion game, played indoors or outdoors, involves throwing and catching as the primary techniques, with tactical principles similar to soccer. Although most students may not know how to play team handball, they do differ in their skills of running, catching, and throwing. Also, students with experience in court or field invasion games will adjust to team handball more quickly because of the tactical similarities. Thus, heterogeneity is likely to be present even in games unfamiliar to nearly all students. In basketball, soccer, and volleyball seasons (that is, sports commonly played in America) the heterogeneity of student backgrounds may be even more pronounced.

Our suggestion is that you consider arranging competitions that allow all students to enjoy the game and be successful. In Sport Education most teachers accomplish this primarily by creating competitions that match students of similar skill levels against one another, what we call graded competition. They have each team assign their players to an A, B, and C level competition. In many situations, this is sufficient to help students learn and enjoy the game through equal competition. What we are suggesting here, however, is that you consider a further refinement of this principle by having the game be somewhat different in each of the competition levels. You can use combinations of any of the modification approaches described earlier in this chapter. Players competing in the A, B, and C competitions might use different balls, sizes of courts, or scoring rules. Students with less experience and lower abilities can play a game in the C competition that they can enjoy and at which they can be successful. Students in the A competition can play a somewhat more challenging game and achieve the same results. What is important is that success in competition counts equally at all levels, so that when C teams play well they contribute as much to the seasonal championship as when A teams play well.

INCLUDING STUDENTS WITH DISABILITIES

You can put in place a number of rule modifications to accommodate students with disabilities. Some specific examples of modifications to promote the success of students with disabilities are provided in figure 5.3. Moreover, the committee or sports board options of Sport Education provide excellent opportunities for students themselves to investigate ways to include students with disabilities into game play. As a general rule, appropriate adjustments include modifying equipment, reducing defensive pressure, eliminating time restrictions, and providing alternate scoring options. The sports board may be asked to not only develop policies of inclusion, but also outline the wording of specific rule modifications. Indeed, in some cases, the sports board may require that certain restrictions be put on able students so they may be more likely to appreciate the special challenges facing those with disabilities.

Suggested Game Modifications

Modify activities to equalize competition.

- Allow a student to kick or hit a stationary ball where it might otherwise be pitched.
- In volleyball, allow them to catch the ball and throw it or allow the ball to bounce.
- Allow a certain length of time to get to base or the goal that is commensurate with the student's abilities.
- Where indoor and outdoor venues are used concurrently, attempt to schedule the games in the gymnasium or on another smooth surface so it is easier for them to get around (e.g., avoid a grassy field).
- Involved the disabled student in making decisions concerning rule modifications.

Decrease distances.

- Move bases closer together.
- Allow students to be closer to the target, goal, or net.
- In volleyball or badminton, allow them to serve from mid-court.

Provide more chances to score.

- Allow three foul shots instead of two; four strikes instead of three; nine arrows instead of six; and so on.

Analyze positions according to the abilities of disabled students.

- Allow them to be goalie, pitcher, or another position entailing limited mobility.
- Allow a student with a heart problem to be goalie in soccer or a pitcher in softball.
- Allow a one-leg amputee to be a pitcher or first baseman.

Provide adapted equipment that makes performance easier such as:

- Larger bat
- Larger, lighter, or softer ball
- Larger, flat bases, goals, baskets, and so on
- Shorter racket shaft or larger racket face

Figure 5.3   Game modifications allow students with special needs to participate and equalize competition.

Reprinted with permission from Granite District Schools, 340 East 3545 South, Salt Lake City, Utah 84115-4697: (801) 263-6100. http://www.granite.k12.ut.us/Special_Ed/homepage.html

CREATING A MODIFIED SPORTS, GAMES, AND ACTIVITIES CURRICULUM

In chapter 2, we outlined our thoughts on developing a Sport Education curriculum. We recognize that most school districts have District Curriculum Syllabi (or Graded Courses of Study as they are sometimes called). In such efforts, physical educators often list many team, dual, and individual sports along with outdoor and adventure activities and often several forms of dance. We suggest that you consider creating a school- or districtwide curriculum that emphasizes modifications of those activities and provides it with some local flavor.

At the outset of this chapter, we made reference to KiwiSport, the national curriculum of modified sports and games that are used in schools, in community recreation, and in sport clubs throughout New Zealand. A similar venture exists in Australia with the AussieSport program. KiwiSport "is all about helping young people develop a great attitude to sport and physical activity. Making it fun, giving everyone a go, giving kids a great sporting start. It's about making sport a habit—and hooking kids for life" (www.sparc.org.nz). We would suggest that these goals are consistent with current goals for physical education in the United States and elsewhere. The KiwiSport program includes a variety of modified sports and activities (see figure 5.4). The great advantage of a national program is that youngsters in New Zealand who play Kiwi cricket in their school physical education program will also play the same game in a community youth sport program and at cricket clubs. The second advantage is that by deciding on forms of modified sports, these nations have been able to produce equipment and rules that

New Zealand National KiwiSport Program

KiwiSport is a national program of sport for children and youth. All sports are modified by smaller playing areas, reduced playing time, modified equipment, simplified rules, and include a primary focus on skill development.

KiwiAuskick	KiwiOrienteering	KiwiVolley
KiwiCycling	KiwiPetanque	KiwiWrestling
KiwiBadminton	KiwiSki	KiwiBasketball
KiwiCricket	KiwiTeeball	KiwiRugby
KiwiGolf	KiwiSquash	KiwiRugby League
KiwiGymfun	KiwiTable Tennis	KiwiMini Hockey
KiwiIndoor Bowls	KiwiTennis	KiwiMini Soccer
KiwiNetball	KiwiTouch	KiwiAthletics
KiwiCroquet	KiwiTri	KiwiTrampoline

More than 90% of all New Zealand elementary and middle schools now offer KiwiSport to their students. KiwiSport is also available in community recreation programs.

KiwiSport coordinators help teachers and coaches deliver KiwiSport.

Figure 5.4 The sports included in the New Zealand national KiwiSport program are played in schools, community recreation programs, and in sport clubs.

Reprinted, by permission, from SPARC, New Zealand.

are appropriate for playing the modified version of the sport. The equipment and rules will be used in school physical education, community recreation programs, as well as in sport clubs.

The beauty of Sport Education is that it is designed to be age appropriate and to utilize the positive aspects of team that create confident, competent, and physically active students. It is truly refreshing to watch a physical education class using Sport Education, because you can actually see students of all physical levels and ages gaining the confidence, knowledge, and social appreciation that are directly linked to sports experiences.

—Columbus School for Girls (Ohio), newsletter to parents

You could easily create a local version of KiwiSport for your school or district. You could use the name of your town, school, or school mascot for the program. For example, Dublin, Ohio is a suburb of Columbus. One of the high schools in Dublin is Dublin Coffman HS. The school nickname is the Shamrocks. A ShamrockSport program could be created with all the modified sports and activities that will be used in the Sport Education program at the high school and its feeder middle and elementary schools. Physical educators could agree on the group of activities and sports to be included, the ways in which they will be modified, and the equipment that will have to be produced or purchased to do them.

A further potential benefit of this approach would be achieved if the physical educators in the district could work with the leaders of the community recreation and youth sport programs to adopt ShamrockSport for those programs also. This would meet all of the requirements we suggest for extending participation described in chapter 11.

"Are we going to play a game today?" How many physical educators hear this question from their students on nearly a daily basis? Most children and youth like games. They especially like games that are friendly, meaning that they can participate successfully and not feel out of place or bewildered by the complexity of the game. Modified games are a key component of Sport Education. In this chapter, we have introduced the different kinds of modifications required for different categories of games. For example, invasion game modifications are different from court-divided modifications, which are different still from sector game modifications. There are endless ways for creative teachers to modify games to meet the particular needs of a diverse group of students. In this chapter we have shown how space, equipment, rules, size of teams, graded competitions, and other strategies can be used to meet local needs.

Chapter **6**

Designing Competition Formats

**14**
Chapter Slides

One of the authors of this book has unpleasant memories of playing on an under-11 soccer team. He came to realize that he had a special role on that team. It was neither goalkeeper nor fullback, sweeper nor striker; it was the 3-goal player. That is, when the team was 3 goals ahead, he would get to play, because the game was well in hand. Likewise, if his team was losing 3 to 0, he also got to play, because the coach decided by that stage the team really had no chance to win. Many people tell equivalent sport stories of children spending more time on the sidelines watching and waiting than they do playing. While an increasing focus exists on participation in both youth sport and physical education, a serious commitment to equal opportunity is seldom present.

In chapter 1, we stated that a primary difference between Sport Education and community and youth sport is a commitment to equal participation. Students not only should get equal playing time but they should have equal opportunity to learn different position play in various activities. This commitment to equal participation is a key factor to consider when designing competition formats, just as the commitment to developmentally appropriate participation was the key factor in modifying the games that would comprise the competition. We begin this chapter on competition formats by explaining three guiding principles for designing competition formats to ensure equal participation.

GUIDING PRINCIPLES

**14**
Chapter Slides

The first guiding principle in designing Sport Education competition formats for equal playing opportunity is that all students get equal opportunity to play. This result can be achieved with small-sided games in which students also get equal opportunity to learn position play. In Sport Education, teams often have no substitutes. When the number of students requires that teams have substitutes, often only one such student exists, and the student is still guaranteed equal playing time. In cases in which teams have one or two players more than the game and competition format allows, you can create substitution rules so that all team members get equal playing time. Chapter 5 described the many ways parent games can be modified to create the small-sided games used in Sport Education. Equal opportunity to play also means that students should learn different position play during the season. The emphasis in interscholastic sport is specialization, where players learn to be point guards, outside hitters, or sweepers. In Sport Education, you should provide students opportunities to learn different position play.

The second guiding principle of competition is an emphasis on the team. All competitions are first and foremost team competitions. Working together toward a common goal is one of the key educational and developmental goals for Sport Education. Teams win a competition and teams win seasonal championships. The seasonal competition format is focused on team performance, even in individual sports such as badminton, swimming, or gymnastics. In these sports individual performances will contribute to an overall team score, grade, or ranking. As a result, the reward and reporting system (i.e., posted league standings) is organized around team performance. Competitions in Sport Education still allow for individual place winners, runners-up, and the like to be recognized. The strongest focus, nonetheless, is the team. The seasonal champion, the best duty team, the team with the most fair play points, or the team with the best offensive or defensive statistics will all be recognized more than an individual scoring leader. The focus on team does not preclude using the Sport Education format for individual sports. On the contrary, they are very suitable for Sport Education, but the competition formats organized for these seasons are team oriented.

Supplementary Materials

The third guiding principle is that competition is graded. We know that competitions are most fun and most useful for learning when they are as evenly matched as possible. Students in any typical physical education class are likely to be very different in terms of previous experience and skill in whatever sport or activity is the focus for a season. We have continuously emphasized the viability of organizing graded competition so that students get to compete against classmates of similar skills and experiences. Indeed, the **research on Sport Education** shows that graded competition produces a number of positive outcomes for less-skilled students and typically nonparticipating students. First, these students claim they develop a sense of belonging and trust from their teammates, and with this, a feeling that is best summarized as "now I think I can." These students believe that they not only can improve in skill, but can also make a positive contribution to their teams (Carlson, 1995; Carlson & Hastie, 1997).

Research has consistently shown that children and youth like contests that are even, where the outcome is uncertain. An uneven contest is no fun for either the winner or loser. This process starts with creation of teams that are as even as possible (see chapter 4). The process continues with the design of the graded competition formats for the season. For example, in a tennis season, a team might have A, B, and C levels for singles players and A and B levels for doubles teams. Students at each level compete against their equivalent rivals from the other teams. Likewise, in a basketball season, you can organize the competition with A- and B-level coed teams, or, alternately, with A and B teams for boys and A and B teams for girls. You can combine these formats for multiple competition seasons so that boys, girls, and coed competitions all count toward the seasonal championship.

A corollary to this idea is that the smaller-sided the game format is, the easier it becomes to create graded competitions. If 3v3 volleyball is the game format for a class of 30 students, you would organize three teams with 10 players on each team. You can arrange a competition format with three levels. It could be A-, B-, and C-level games. It also could be boys, girls, and coed games.

The remainder of this chapter focuses on six general formats that you can use to design suitable competition in Sport Education. Table 6.1 gives a summary of how these competition formats will operate.

Table 6.1   General Principles and Variations of Different Competition Formats

Competition format	General principles	Variations
Progressive competition seasons	Use the same sport throughout. Add more tactical and technical complexity as the competitions change. Team and place winners from each of the competitions contribute to the seasonal championship.	All students compete in a basic skills competition to begin, then move to various levels as the season progresses.
Event model	Students compete in events by themselves but all their performances count toward a team collective score.	Have relay competitions. Have individual performances with students being placed in different events. Have individual performances with students placed in different divisions (e.g., weightlifting). Have multi-event competitions.
Dual meet model	Students compete in singles or doubles competition against those from another team. Teams add all match scores to determine the winner for the day.	Have singles, doubles, and mixed doubles from each team. Start with doubles competition, then progress to singles competition.
Round robin	All teams play against each other during a season.	Have a dual round robin, with the first being a practice for the second. For classes with large numbers of teams, have different conferences.
Tournament	Teams play against each other depending on their results from previous matches.	Create a compass tournament. Create a bumper board tournament. Create a pyramid tournament.
Tabloids	Teams rotate throughout a circuit with rankings at each circuit counting toward the final placement.	Have weekly challenges.

PROGRESSIVE COMPETITION FORMATS

14
Chapter Slides

You can use the **progressive competition format** in a number of ways. The purpose of the format is to have a series of competitions that become tactically and technically more advanced. For example, for a season of soccer, the series might begin with a 1v1 competition, followed by a 2v2, then a 4v4 competition. You should grade these mini-team competitions by skill and experience so that students of similar abilities compete against each other. Each successive competition is designed to allow for introducing more complex techniques and tactics. It is always helpful to begin the season with a scrimmage (a game that does not count toward the championship) so that students can learn the organizational and duty team responsibilities as well as become acquainted with the competition format (e.g., small-sided teams, timed games). Figure 6.1 shows a sample competition format. You can also find this figure on the accompanying CD-ROM.

6
Progressive Competition Format

Season Phase 1 Teams

Players' rank	Blazers	Flyers	Kings	Rockies	Grizzlies
1	Charlie	Elizabeth	Pedro	Tom	Raoul
2	Missy	Sasha	Angela	Dave	Paula
3	Desi	Paul	Han	Russell	Mia
4	Jim	Reed	Shelly	Clarice	Roger
5	Lisa	Roger	Vladii	Beth	Alan
6	Mary	Kevin	Neil	Seth	Ping

Players ranked within teams based on performance during pre-season scrimmages.

Season Phase 2 Teams

Players' rank		Blazers	Flyers	Kings	Rockies	Grizzlies
1 6	A	Charlie / Mary	Elizabeth / Kevin	Pedro / Neil	Tom / Seth	Raoul / Ping
2 5	B	Missy / Lisa	Sasha / Roger	Angela / Vladii	Dave / Beth	Paula / Alan
3 4	C	Desi / Jim	Paul / Reed	Han / Shelly	Russell / Clarice	Mia / Roger

Figure 6.1   Sample progressive competition format.

You can also build the progressive competition format around changes in the size of the competition space, the nature of the implements and balls, and other features that make the particular sport or activity progressively more advanced. For example, a beginning competition in tennis might use shorter rackets, softer balls, and a service line closer to the net. As students get more experienced and confident, a subsequent competition can change any or all of those features.

In this format, you will have team and place winners from each of the competitions that have contributed to the season championships. For example, in the soccer example just described, the Devils may have scored the most total points in the 1v1 competition, while the Eagles may have had the greatest success in the 3v3 or 4v4 competitions.

This progressive format is not limited to team sports such as volleyball or floor hockey. For example, you may develop a gymnastics model in which students will compete in progressively more complex activities (Bell, 1994). Early in the season, a compulsory floor exercise competition may take place. The competition would have an A and a B level for routines. Teams would first practice at their home mats, with captains acting as demonstrators, and with the emphasis being on the development of technique. Students would work on techniques and also develop a routine that conformed to required routine elements. As in team sports, you could hold a scrimmage-like event in which students performed and also learned their duty team roles, which might include judging in this case.

When the floor exercise competition is completed, the next phase of the season might focus on apparatus competitions, such as balance beam, parallel bars, and vaulting. In this phase also, you could have different levels of competition. Students would create a routine for their apparatus and level of competition. Students would not only be scored on their skills, but on transitions, contrasts, and expression.

A third phase of the season might focus on acrosport with students creating various building configurations involving various numbers of students. You might use this portion of the season as the culminating event with students' pyramids videotaped and students having created costumes. A summary of the progressive competition format is shown in table 6.2.

Table 6.2 Progressive Competition Format

Content progression	Keys to note
Techniques and skills of 1v1 play	Teach organization for 1v1 scrimmages.
1v1 competition	Duty team players referee or coach. Teach techniques and tactics such as forward and defender.
2v2 competition	Scorekeepers can begin to keep simple performance statistics. You can introduce various position combinations, such as forwards and defenders, or a specialist position such as goalkeeper.
3v3 or 4v4 competitions	Games will now consist of 6-8 players with 2 referees and 2 scorekeepers.
6v6 competitions	Results from this section of the competition do not usually count toward the final team championship.

EVENT MODEL

In the event model, students compete in events by themselves, but all their performances count toward a team collective score. During the earliest part of a season, students work on developing the techniques and fitness levels required for successful participation in competition. For example, track athletes practice their starts, their hurdle techniques, or their pacing skills. Swimmers develop sufficient endurance to allow them to complete their events while at the same time learning and refining their strokes, turns, and starts.

In the early stages of this **event format,** competition is often limited to intrasquad events, whereby coaches will help their team members determine who will represent the team in the various events. The bulk of the season focuses on a series of team competitions. During the later part of the season, teams come together in a celebratory event to contest the final championships. How many days you allocate

to these final championships will depend on the number of events to be completed. For example, in a cross country season (which might include both walking and running competitions), all events may be completed in just one day, with final races of different distances, following a season where races have been previously held over different distances. For track and field, three days may be required for the culminating event, with the first day for throwing events, the second day for running events, and the final day for jumping events. During the final championships, teams would be expected to provide both athletes and officials. You may ask for nominations from officials to cover all events (e.g., one for each gymnastics event) or you may allocate one event team (e.g., the high jump) to a specific team.

Relay Competitions

One option for the event format is to have students compete strictly in a competition of relays. In this case, individual performances are replaced by a collective team time or score. This relay format is especially appropriate to sports such as swimming, cross country, and track and field. You could include shuttle hurdle relays, shot put collective distance, as well as 400 m and 800 m relay teams.

Individual Performance With Students Placed in Different Events

Within a team, athletes may compete in a single event (e.g., the floor exercises in gymnastics), or may contest more than one (e.g., the 100 m dash and the long jump in track and field). Depending on the total number of team members, the individual workload of the athletes will vary. In large teams, an athlete may be able to specialize (e.g., swim the 800 m freestyle only), while in small teams, athletes may be required to double up, or compete in three or more events. In sports such as track and field, it is important that all students have a chance to learn techniques for all events. Thus, in competitions during the season they may compete in running, throwing, and jumping events. In the culminating event of a two- or three-day championship, you might ask teams to have each team member compete in at least two of those three types of events.

Individual Performance With Students Placed in Different Divisions

This variation is useful for situations in which performance is affected by size and strength (e.g., weightlifting). In this variation, all team members will compete in the same events (e.g., bench press, clean, and squat), but against people in their same weight division. Weekly challenges are used as mini-competitions during the season, and individual team members keep personal record sheets of their workouts and lifts. Sweeney, Tannehill, and Teeters (1992) described a Sport Education strength training season for high school girls. A class of 31 girls was divided into seven teams. Four weight divisions determined the pool of students to be assigned to each team. Class A was 96 to 109 pounds, class B was 112 to 119 pounds, class C was 121 to 134 pounds, and class D was 135 pounds and over. Weekly challenges were held, leading to a final competition. The final competition was a team event in which the total weight lifted by a team across all events and weight divisions was used to determine the competition champion. An alternative to this last method is to add the placings to create a team total.

Multi-Event Meet

In a multi-event meet, teams can elect to send one or more athlete representatives to any one of the events being conducted during the competition. A team may chose to send three or even four athletes to one event, while ignoring another completely. However, all teams must send at least two representatives to act as officials to the events as designated by the teacher. In this multi-event format, you can cover more events in a season, and teams can have more flexibility.

An example of a multi-event meet in gymnastics would be a competition where six apparatuses (beam, short vault, floor, horizontal bar, hoops, and four-person pyramid) are available. Officials at each station will take entries, determine a competition order, and judge performances, while athletes from each team can participate in any one event.

Table 6.3   Event Model (Variation 1)

Content progression	Keys to note
Techniques and fitness development	Teach techniques of different events.
No-consequence challenges	Two teams will contest an event while a third team provides the officials.
Specialized practice	
Specialized competition	Teams select representatives and officials to different events.
Carnival	Each team is responsible for officiating one event.

Table 6.4   Event Model (Variation 2)

Content progression	Keys to note
Techniques and fitness development	Teach techniques of different events.
No-consequence challenges	Two teams will contest an event while a third team provides the officials.
Skill 1 relay	Cumulative scores of all team members provide a total; team rankings count toward season championship.
Skill 2 relay	Continue with weekly challenges.
Final skill relay	The number of relays depends on the number of events to be contested at the carnival.
Carnival	Each team is responsible for officiating one event.

DUAL-MEET FORMAT

Dual meets take place between two teams, each of whom is represented by a number of individuals or pairs. Each of these individuals or pairs will compete against an equivalent individual or pair from their opponents. A third team will complete the duty responsibilities for this match.

The team that accrues the most total wins over the course of these contests is declared the winner of the **dual-meet season,** but may or may not win the overall

6
Dual Meet Format

seasonal championship award based on points for fair play, duty team performance, and the like. Where the number of matches won by each team is even, you can use a next-level tiebreaker of total games (or even total points).

Competitions in tennis, badminton, racquetball, pickleball, or 10-pin bowling often use this format. Depending on the length of each lesson or the total season, players may participate in singles and doubles competition. For shorter seasons, the competition may consist of two singles and two doubles matches. For longer seasons, you may hold two competitions—first a doubles and then a singles. Alternately, each competition could consist of both singles and doubles. See table 6.5 for a summary of the dual-meet format.

Table 6.5   Dual-Meet Format

Content progression	Keys to note
Techniques and skills of play	Conduct skills practices and begin teaching officiating.
Intrasquad matches	Teams play short games to determine team representation; self-officiated.
First round of competitions with selected format (e.g., 2 singles players and 2 doubles teams from each team contest against similar opponents)	Introduce duty teams with scorekeepers keeping simple performance statistics.
Second round of competition	May change the team organization (e.g., introduce mixed doubles).
Championships	Have small tournaments between all players within the same skill bracket counting toward an overall team champion.

ROUND-ROBIN FORMAT

Round-Robin

In the round-robin format, all teams play against each other during a season. On any given competition day (see chapter 4), using the small-sided, timed-games format, all teams are likely to play and, of course, all teams will have duty team responsibilities. The scope of a **round-robin** tournament depends entirely on the number of teams and the levels of graded competition within teams. For example, in a class of 32 with three teams of 10 to 11 students per team, you might have at least two and possibly three levels of graded competition (three teams within each of the large teams). With three levels of competition, each level of the round-robin competition would require three games to complete, thus nine games to complete competition at each of the three levels. Using the same class size, but dividing the 32 students into five teams with six to seven students per team and two levels of competition, you would need 10 games for each level, or 20 total games to complete the round robin.

One of the organizational dilemmas of round-robin competition occurs when one class has a large number of teams. For example, an eight-team competition will require 28 matches for all teams to play each other just with one level of competition. To overcome this challenge, many teachers choose to have a number of divisions or pools within a class. After competition against all the teams in the

Round-Robin

same conference or division, teams will then compete against similarly ranked teams from the other conferences in a series of play-offs. Hence, an eight-team league playing in two divisions will only require a total of 12 games before play-offs, while a 10-team league will now require but 20 games. Figure 6.2 shows an example of such a format with eight teams of four players. You can also find this figure on the accompanying CD-ROM.

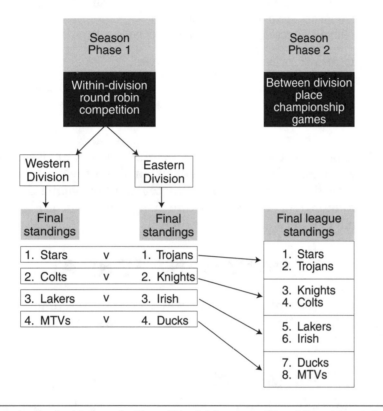

Figure 6.2 Sample round-robin format with a within-division competition, followed by a between-division competition.

Teachers constantly expressed amazement at the improvements in the quality of games as seasons progressed. It is evident that the benefits of the games-based learning make Sport Education far superior to the traditional teaching model.

—Sport Ed II SPARC 1994

An alternate to the round-robin format is to include two competitions within one season, which can be a variation of the **progressive competition format** described earlier in that the second round-robin competition is a slightly more complex game from a technical and tactical perspective. Alternately, the first round-robin competition can act as a prelude for the second. Between the two competitions, teams will spend time reviewing their performance, discussing team needs, and practicing selected skills or plays. In some cases, the second round-robin competition will involve rule modifications from the first season, based on the your observations

Progressive Competition Format

Table 6.6 Round-Robin Format

Content progression	Keys to note
Techniques and skills	Teach skills, rules, and officiating.
Preseason competition/first round-robin competition	Use duty teams, with scorekeepers beginning to keep simple performance statistics. Games are of no consequence with regard to the season champions. Teach more advanced techniques and tactics. Teach more advanced statistics or make rule modifications.
Main competition/second round-robin competition	Duty teams will conduct all administrative roles. Games count toward competition rankings.
Culminating event	Have festive games against teams of similar ranking, or those from other classes.

or on decisions made by the class sports board. With larger classes using pool or divisional play, you also need to make a decision about the composition of teams for the second section. In other words, will teams play against those same ones from the first round-robin competition, or will new divisions be created? Table 6.6 shows a summary of the round-robin format.

TOURNAMENT FORMAT

The tournament format offers another way to structure competitions. We will highlight three tournament structures: the compass, pyramid, and ladder (or bumper) formats.

Tournament Format

Compass Tournaments

The **compass tournament format** (see figure 6.3) has the teams seeded. For example, in the first round Team 1 plays Team 2, Team 3 plays Team 4, Team 5 plays Team 6, and Team 7 plays Team 8. (This format accommodates large numbers of teams—the eight-team format is used only as an example.) The first-round winners move to an Eastern Division while the first-round losing teams move to a Western Division. (Division designations could be of any variety; e.g., Red/White/Blue/Green). Second-round losers move to a new division where they play a Championship game for that division. Second-round winners move to a Championship game for that division.

Tournament Format

Ladder and Pyramid Tournaments

Ladder and **pyramid tournaments** are cousins in that they both involve lower-ranked teams challenging higher-ranked teams. Teachers, perhaps in consultation with captains or a sports board, create tournament rules and regulations. If a team on a lower level (pyramid) or rung (ladder) challenges and defeats a team two rungs above, the teams trade places on the chart. Both ladders and pyramids could be created for different levels of skill in a class (e.g., an A, B, and C ladder or a boys, girls, and coed ladder). In this model, duty teams are assigned ahead of time, so that for that day or a portion of that day, duty teams will be unable to issue challenges (see figure 6.4).

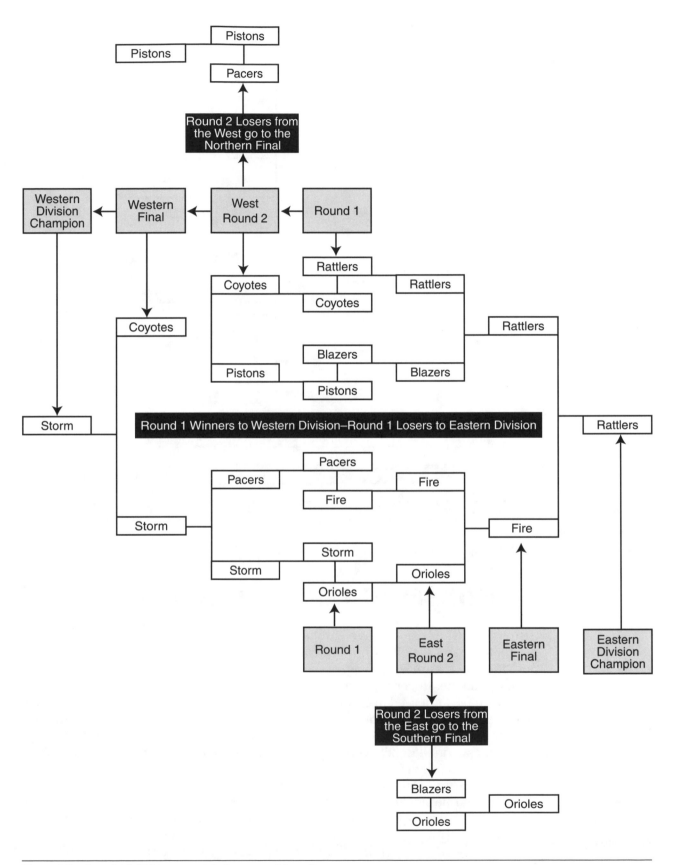

Figure 6.3 Sample eight-team compass tournament format.

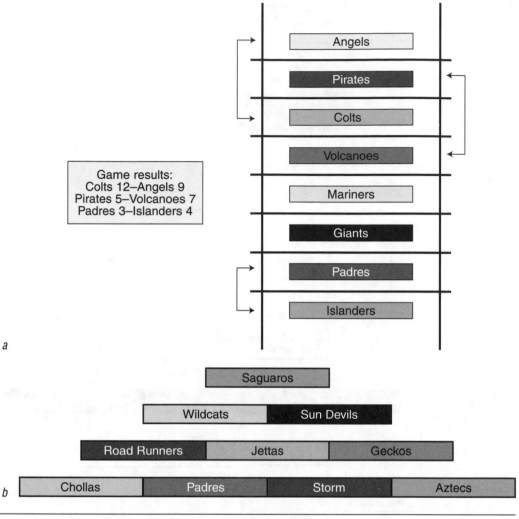

Game results:
Colts 12–Angels 9
Pirates 5–Volcanoes 7
Padres 3–Islanders 4

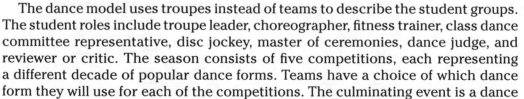

Figure 6.4   *(a)* Sample ladder and *(b)* pyramid tournament formats.

NONSPORT COMPETITION FORMATS

Throughout the text we have emphasized that you can use the Sport Education model for many activities not typically considered to be sports; that is, outdoor activities such as orienteering, exercise activities such as aerobics, and the many forms of dance. Recently, two approaches to organizing Sport Education dance seasons have appeared in the literature (Graves & Townsend, 2000; Richardson & Oslin, 2003). Table 6.7 shows a 21-session schedule for a dance season, adapted from the model described by Graves and Townsend (2000). Various roles for the dance season include: choreographer, fitness trainer, dance committee member, disc jockey, master of ceremonies, judge, and reviewer/critic.

The dance model uses troupes instead of teams to describe the student groups. The student roles include troupe leader, choreographer, fitness trainer, class dance committee representative, disc jockey, master of ceremonies, dance judge, and reviewer or critic. The season consists of five competitions, each representing a different decade of popular dance forms. Teams have a choice of which dance form they will use for each of the competitions. The culminating event is a dance

Sample Season Block Plans

Table 6.7 Seasonal Schedule for Popular Dance

Day	Focus
1	Form dance troupes (teams); explain roles; review handout listing dances from various eras. Show videos of selected dances.
2	Troupes decide who will fulfill various roles; troupes are introduced to elementary dance techniques and rituals and traditions of dance.
3-5	1950s dances introduced and practiced; troupes begin to plan for 1950s dance competition (music and dance); schedule of dance competitions is posted; judging is introduced.
6	1950s dance competition.
7-9	Troupes practice dance they will perform in 1960s competition.
10	1960s dance competition.
11-13	Troupes practice dance they will perform in 1970s competition.
14	1970s dance competition.
15-17	Troupes practice dance they will perform in 1980s competition.
18	1980s dance competition.
19-21	Troupes practice dance they will perform in 1990s competition.
22	1990s dance competition.
23	Dance festival and awards celebration.

Adapted from model suggested by Graves & Townsend (2000).

festival with each troupe picking the dance they most liked and performing it again for the class.

CULMINATING EVENTS

All authentic sporting experiences end with a culminating event. The Super Bowl and the World Cup soccer final draw millions of viewers across the world. Most junior leagues, too, have some activity that culminates the season.

In Sport Education, the end-of-season event represents the culmination of the sporting experience with one critical difference. In most sport systems, only the two best teams get to participate in this final activity. In Sport Education, the focus is on festivity and full participation of all teams. Both competitive and social outcomes are celebrated and shared among the students in the class.

The end-of-season event need not be only on the final day of the competition round. You can spread championships and other end-of-season competitions over several days. While you may have a championship game in a tournament, you should have third-, fifth-, seventh-, and ninth-place games as well. The culminating celebration should include more than just the promotion of the competition winners. You can provide awards or recognition that focus on fair play, on the contribution that students have made to their roles, or to individual contributions to the season as a whole or to their teams. You can show videotapes of championship contests. These culminating events are an integral part of making the sport experience festive for all students. (See chapter 10 for strategies for making seasons and culminating events festive.)

The Format of Culminating Events

Culminating Events/One-Day Skill Challenges

Culminating events can take many forms. Some classes treat the occasion as purely a social one, while others include some activity relating to the season's competition, where teams compete against each other in a series of technique or **skill challenges.** In all cases, you need to consider cost, venue, outside and special guests, and duration. In some seasons, the sports board has raised money for the presentations. The money went toward providing awards and for catering the class party. In other seasons, teams were able to conduct their festive day's competitions at an elite sporting venue, one not otherwise available for public use. Some sport councils have invited the local press to their celebrations and have garnered newspaper coverage of the final day's activities. Others have produced highlights videos and shown them together with a special guest speaker at a special players' breakfast. Through a negotiation between the physical education and classroom staff, the culminating events of some seasons have extended beyond the regular time allocated for physical education.

In all cases, the culminating event needs to be a planned and purposeful experience. It should not take on the form of an afterthought; it should be an event that enhances the entire season. In the planning phases, many teachers have found that students are more than willing to take responsibility for organizing the various components to develop a truly celebratory occasion.

Another way to add to the sense of festivity without sacrificing time or money is to hold inter-divisional finals (i.e., for overall first, third, and fifth place) during open gym or lunchtime periods. With added publicity, you could invite the entire student body to attend the championship games.

A Final Word on Awards

Awards

There is almost no limit to the **awards** and the format of those awards that can be given at the culmination of a sport education season. As noted, because a sport education season seeks to achieve a number of goals beyond skillful play, the awards should reflect those goals. While it is certainly legitimate to honor the most outstanding team, you should also award other components of a season such as fair play, committee membership, skill improvement, and teamwork (see also chapter 8).

Different competitions take differing amounts of class time. We have attempted to describe a range of formats from which you can choose. We have also made it clear why and how all competitions should involve all students equally. We tried to show how arranging graded competitions makes for a better and more enjoyable learning and competing experience for students. In chapter 1 we described our views on the appropriate nature of competitions for Sport Education. Developmentally appropriate competition is a fundamentally important characteristic of Sport Education. Designing the appropriate format is the link that allows students to have beneficial competitive experiences.

Chapter **7**

Class Management
and Behavior Development

Sport Education encourages and relies on student involvement, responsibility, and leadership. Because Sport Education relies on responsible student involvement in various phases of the season, goals for effective class management and positive behavior development are very important. The student-centered nature of Sport Education also makes some approaches to class management and behavior development more appropriate than others. For example, in one approach teachers are always in full, direct control of the class and the primary and sometimes sole role of the student is to comply with teacher directions and class behavior rules. While this approach might work for some PE teaching methods, it is not consistent with the goals and strategies of Sport Education.

Chapter Slides

Sport Education aims to build student responsibility and leadership and to help students learn to manage and direct their own sport experiences. In Sport Education teachers gradually empower students to be responsible team members and to acquit themselves responsibly in a number of leadership roles that are crucial to the success of each season. Classes will not run smoothly unless coaches and managers do their jobs well. Seasonal competitions will not be successful unless referees, scorekeepers, and statisticians do their jobs well. Sport Education also emphasizes being a supportive teammate, participating enthusiastically, and playing fairly. The goal in Sport Education is to move the relationship between teacher and students, and among students, from compliance to cooperation and eventually to community (Siedentop & Tannehill, 2000).

Many teachers prefer to make this transition gradually, although evidence in the Sport Education literature suggests that some teachers move immediately from direct control to a full student-centered approach (Grant, 1992). For the many PE teachers who have already developed management and behavior systems in which students cooperate with the teacher to sustain an effective class system and atmosphere, the move to Sport Education will be a smooth one. We believe that when Sport Education is done well, classes take on the characteristics of a learning community.

**Supplemental
Resources/Research
on Sport Education**

> A learning community exists when students feel valued, feel they are supported by their teacher and classmates, are connected to one another, and are committed to each other's learning, growth and welfare. . . . Learning communities have specific characteristics that take time and effort to develop. Learning communities are bounded

environments that persist over time. Members share important common goals, and they cooperate to achieve those goals. They share allegiance to significant symbols and take part together in rituals that emphasize their community. (Siedentop & Tannehill, 2000, p. 98)

In Sport Education, the formation of heterogeneous teams is the key feature that enables the development of community during the seasons making up a school year. For the seasons to be successful, team members have to cooperate to achieve collective goals. Each team also has to cooperate with other teams to make the season work. Loyalty and support become important to each team's success. Eventually, the class itself can become a learning community. All of the Sport Education goals identified in chapter 1 are easier to achieve when teachers adopt management and behavior strategies that lead toward cooperation and community. We first address class management strategies and then behavior development.

> *T*his module promotes a more one-on-one learning basis for team members, while it also teaches everyone about the aspect of the sport which is lacking in the usual PE course. There is team participation and pride in the team.
>
> —Tenth grade student, New Zealand

Chapter Slides

CLASS MANAGEMENT TECHNIQUES AND TACTICS

Sport Education seasons are longer than traditional PE units because students are expected to learn more content and roles. They are also expected to learn techniques and tactics to a sufficiently high level that they feel motivated to continue to participate. Time is a precious commodity in Sport Education. It is important to use the available time as wisely and productively as possible so students can have the maximum time allowable to learn and improve. Also, many disruptive behavior problems occur during those times in class when students are not engaged productively, whether during managerial chores such as starting class and changing activities or in instructional episodes such as technique drills. In other words, students will use the down time to find something to do, and that something may prove to be disruptive to the class and require your attention. The approach in Sport Education is to practice preventive class management, which "refers to the proactive (rather than reactive) strategies teachers use to develop and maintain a positive, predictable, task-oriented class climate in which minimal time is devoted to managerial tasks and optimal time is therefore available for instructional tasks" (Siedentop & Tannehill, 2000, p. 61). The overall goal of a preventive class management system is to develop and sustain regular, predictable procedures for students to accomplish those segments and elements of class that recur with regularity.

Important Class Segment Routines

You should create routines for all the important managerial episodes used in the typical class session. Routines specify the procedures used in class to get a specific management task done quickly and well. Creating a predictable flow of class time is likely to require routines for entry into the activity space and home bases, transitions between segments of the lesson, equipment changes, and lesson closure. These episodes are discussed next.

Entry Into the Activity Space and Home Bases

When students arrive at the activity space, they should become immediately engaged in activities that contribute to lesson goals. First, students should have assigned spaces to go to when they arrive. In Sport Education, these spaces are typically team spaces. Whether inside or outside, each team should have a designated portion of the space that is their home field for the duration of a season. In gyms, you can designate spaces by posting **team banners** along walls. When students arrive they can immediately go to their space and begin to do the assigned activity, with captains or fitness specialists as leaders. You can designate outside spaces with cones or other team markers, such as sections of a lined field. Whenever teams warm up, do technique drills, or meet to decide competition strategies, they should do so in their team space.

Home Field Banners

Routines for arrival at the space will likely differ according to school level. At the elementary level, students are likely to move from their classroom to the activity space as a group. When students enter and disperse to their home fields, they can begin a warm-up or a technique drill quickly. Teachers have had good success guiding this entry and initial activity routine through use of posters or audiotapes. If the initial activity is a sport-specific warm-up, you can list the activities of the warm-up on the poster or verbalize them on the tape. If a warm-up is followed quickly by a technique practice segment, you can also list the various practice tasks on a poster or control them verbally on an audio tape. (At the end of class you rewind the tape to have it ready for the next class or change the tape if the class or activity is different.) Coaches provide the leadership and supervision of these initial class segments. If you decide to have fitness leader as one of the student roles, this girl or boy would lead the warm-up or fitness activity. You can also use this time to record attendance, if you are required to do so. Team managers or coaches can be assigned the responsibility to report absentees to you immediately following the warm-up. These entry routines will allow you the freedom to interact and support your students rather than spending all your time in the role of traffic cop.

At the high school level, students are likely to come from a locker room at different times before the official start of class. In these cases, students should move immediately to their home field and begin a routine technique drill. Technique drills used in these opening segments should be ones that students know how to do from previous classes, can do with high levels of success, and contribute to ongoing technique refinement. At the official start time for class, teams can begin the fitness or warm-up activity led by their coach or fitness specialist.

Transitions Between Segments of the Lesson

Lesson segments may include warm-up, technique practice, tactical practice, scrimmages, team or class meetings, role practice (e.g., practicing refereeing and scorekeeping), games, cool-down, and closure. Although the number of segments will differ from class to class and as the season progresses, all classes will include some subset of these segments. Each lesson will require smooth transitions among segments, such as moving from technique practice to a controlled scrimmage, changing teams for a new round of competition, moving from a gymnasium to an outside playing field, or gathering as a class for a closure segment. When transitions occur smoothly and quickly, many good things result; namely, the energy of the class is positive, available time is used productively, opportunities for disruptions are minimized, and all planned activities get to be completed. When transitions break down, lessons can seldom be completed as planned, students get frustrated, and disruptions are more likely to occur.

Routines for transitions include a signal for attention, clear instructions, a signal for dispersal into the routine, and an emphasis on completing the transition quickly and without disruption. For example, at the end of a warm-up and technique segment that starts a class, a seventh grade teacher blows her whistle, after which all students immediately stop what they are doing and face her. The teacher then indicates that the first 3v3 soccer scrimmage will come next with the Tomcat teams playing Wolves teams and the Jets as the **duty team.** The scrimmage helps teams practice tactical strategies while duty team members practice refereeing and scorekeeping. The teacher then says, "Go!" The **coaches** for the two competing teams, already in their home space, gather their teams to make sure that the three different three-person team assignments are understood, and the **team manager** quickly shows which of the soccer pitches each team will play on. The duty team coach and **manager** make sure that **referee** and **scorekeeper** assignments are clear and hand out the whistles, statistics sheets, and soccer balls that will be used at each venue. The teacher circulates to make sure that things go smoothly but does not interfere unless she sees a clear disturbance or a team coach makes a request.

Sport Education lessons often include multiple, small-sided, timed games. It is not unusual to have a series of three to five of these multiple games in one lesson. For example, a volleyball season with three class teams might be in the 2v2 portion of their progressive competition season. On this day there will be three game segments. During each segment there would be four 2v2 games lasting five minutes. In each segment two of the teams would compete while the third team has duty team roles. While the **captains** and managers of each of the competing teams are responsible for making sure that members of their teams get to the proper space for their competition, it is the duty team that makes sure that each competition space has a referee and scorekeeper, along with the appropriate equipment. The referee becomes responsible for seeing that the new games begin on time. The transitions among these game segments of a lesson must go smoothly and quickly or the final games on the day's schedule will not have enough time and students will be frustrated. Many teachers have had success teaching this transition as a two-minute drill. From the end of one game segment to the beginning of the next game segment, the competing teams and duty team will have completed all their transition duties in a two-minute time span. The rewards, of course, are the teacher's approval and getting the next game started on schedule so that the full complement of games can be played during that class period.

Equipment Changes

Sport Education most often requires the use of equipment. Students typically have to share equipment. Equipment sometimes changes throughout the course of a lesson. An equipment routine will teach students how to change and exchange equipment. Team managers will play a pivotal role in making sure that team members participate appropriately in any equipment change or exchange. Equipment routines should include specific details about where equipment is to be stored or exchanged and how that equipment is to be treated.

Class Closure

Many teachers like to have a formal closure to class, to provide feedback, to recognize good performance, to provide instructions about the next lesson, and

3
Student Roles/
Student Role Cards

to properly quiet the students so they may return to the classroom. The closure serves many purposes in Sport Education. You can recognize fair play, note improvement, give group feedback on performance, review and reinforce tactical or technical aspects of performance, and strengthen and celebrate the class community. Closure requires that students gather in one place from a dispersed area, get to the closure space quickly, and be organized in a manner that allows them to participate in closure events. The closure routine should also include procedures for leaving the space, removing any equipment, and returning to the locker room or classroom. As with all routines, the specifics of the closure routine need to be taught and practiced. Once you have taught and practiced these routines, students will become accustomed to them and you can use them throughout the school year for various Sport Education seasons.

Important Teacher–Student Interaction Routines

In most classes, you sometimes need to gain the attention of the class, and students need to gather at one place and then be dispersed to participation spaces. You cannot always predict when these routines will be needed, but when they are needed it is important that they happen quickly and without disruption. The most common routines that enable teachers and students to cooperate for lesson success are an attention/quiet routine, a gather routine, a dispersal routine, and a gain attention routine. These routines are particularly important for younger students and for those first learning to do the Sport Education model. We cannot stress enough the importance of ensuring that students get informed about these routines, have opportunities to practice them, and receive feedback on how they perform them.

We use the term *routine* because the procedures for accomplishing any of these managerial goals must become second-nature to the students. You must clearly specify the procedures, and students have to be given the opportunities to practice them. By taking time to specify procedures at the start of the school year, you will save yourself a lot of quality time and prevent a lot of potential disruption the entire school year.

Attention/Quiet Routine

Often during lessons you need to gain the attention of all the students. You should have a clear signal that is the attention signal and you should teach students the expected response to that signal. For example, with younger students, you might want to use a "freeze" signal and the students then stand still, face you, and put any ball or implement they are holding on the floor. Some teachers have had success with a routine that requires students to respond; for example, the teacher signals with a double hand clap, and students respond with a double hand clap as they face the teacher and become quiet. With older students, you can discuss the routine and use student input to decide what the signal might be and what the student response should be. It is consistent with the goals of Sport Education that as students gain experience with the model that they be brought into the decision-making process in many ways.

Gather Routine

Sometimes you need students to gather from dispersed spaces to a specified common space. The gather routine will use the attention/quiet signal and then a simple request to gather. Students should know what to do with equipment (leave it at the dispersed space or bring it with them to the gathering space). You can time early opportunities to use the gather routine, then give specific feedback and establish a new goal to reduce the time taken to gather.

Dispersal Routine

Once gathered, students are typically dispersed to either competition spaces or their home field. It is important that dispersal information include clear instructions about what is to happen once students reach their assigned space. A dispersal signal should indicate when students are to leave the gathered space. In early stages of learning the model, you should time the dispersal from the moment the signal is given until the time the next activity begins at the dispersed spaces. Not only can you verbally commend students who disperse quickly, but you can also add such efforts to the seasonal point scheme and award points with the time needed for dispersal gradually reducing as students become accustomed to move quickly and organize effectively. It is essential as well that teams, once they arrive at their team space, start their warm-up or practice immediately. They should not have to wait for further instructions from you.

Gaining Attention Routine

Finally, it is especially important with younger students that you teach an attention-gaining routine. Students should have access to you, but attention should be gained through a routine that does not disrupt the rest of the team or class. Because younger children are often strongly reinforced by a teacher's attention, they will sometimes use inappropriate means to gain that attention. You must be very careful not to inadvertently reinforce inappropriate attention-getting behavior. The gaining attention routine will show the appropriate way or ways that students should use to gain attention and allow the teacher to give feedback to the student about whether the matter brought to the teacher's attention was appropriate for using the routine. For example, with elementary students the routine might be for a student to stand still and raise a hand high in the air. While somewhat less important as students get older, you should also teach this routine in middle and high school classes in an age-appropriate manner so that students do not compete for attention and disrupt the class.

Game- or Contest-Specific Routines

You should also create routines to help play continue smoothly in games and contests. Two such routines are the boundary and retrieve routines (Siedentop & Tannehill, 2000). The main purpose of these routines is to prevent disruptions by students not assigned to the particular space or field.

Boundary Routine

The boundary routine is especially important for younger children. Its purpose is to teach students to stay within prescribed bounded spaces so that they do not interrupt the participation of other students in adjacent bounded spaces. Many teachers have also included the concepts of self-space and general space when teaching children to stay within their own boundaries and respect the participation of other students in adjacent boundaries. The purpose of this routine is to provide students with a clear sense of what is out of bounds for their own involvement in an activity.

Retrieve Routine

The retrieve routine is similar in purpose but involves the movement of balls rather than people. Often with adjacent soccer pitches or volleyball courts, balls from one game will fly or roll into an adjacent pitch or court. The retrieve routine sets up a procedure in which the ball can be retrieved and returned to the appropriate court with minimal disruption of the play in the adjacent pitch or court. The retrieve routine typically specifies that the ball should be picked up by one of the players into whose space it has come and returned quickly by rolling it on the ground to the space from which it came; that is, the players in the space from which the ball came should not themselves move into the adjacent space to retrieve the ball.

DEVELOPING APPROPRIATE BEHAVIOR: TOWARD A CULTURE OF FAIR PLAY

It has been clear for many years that inadequate discipline is a major deterrent to achieving class goals. Very few good things happen when classes are rowdy, disobedient, and uncooperative. Both research and the wisdom of practice agree that developing and sustaining an orderly, civil environment is crucial to achievement. Sport Education works best when students cooperate, support one another, participate enthusiastically, and act responsibly in all their roles. In this section we focus on strategies for achieving that kind of student involvement.

Sport enthusiasts and professional physical educators have long argued that participation in sport and physical education can positively influence social behavior development. Unfortunately, at least for physical education, little evidence shows that students learn much about cooperation, perseverance, responsibility, and other such laudable social and character objectives. Many have long believed that sports build character, and many athletes have testified that their sport participation helped them to develop self-control, learn teamwork and leadership, and learn to work for deferred consequences. But sport is a two-edged sword. While it can contribute to such positive development, it also can teach and reinforce selfishness, rule breaking, and gaining unfair advantage.

While physical education has emphasized social and character development objectives for more than one hundred years (Siedentop, 2004), the tacit assumption underlying these objectives is that they accrue nearly automatically from participating in sport and other physical activities. It seems obvious that for sport experiences to be a vehicle for social and personal development, the experiences must be significant and substantial; that is, a boring or insignificant experience is not likely to influence social development. Sport Education is designed to provide experiences that are significant and substantial. Therefore, it creates the context within which students can learn valuable personal and social lessons. It is up to the teacher and students, working together, to take advantage of the opportunities that the context provides.

The social and personal development objectives for Sport Education are more specific than in traditional PE, because they are given specific meaning by the context of sport. The long-term goals of Sport Education to develop competent, literate, and enthusiastic sportspersons (see chapter 1) provide guidance for that specificity, as do the formats of teams and seasons. Students learn what it means to be **a leader** as well as a supportive teammate. Students learn exactly what fair play means in the context of specific sports—what are appropriate ways to treat

teammates, opponents, and officials, as well as the importance of playing by the rules to ensure a fair contest and a worthy winner. Because they all experience the role of referee or umpire, students have the chance to learn how it feels to perform in that role and how much good performance in that role contributes to the quality of the competition. Students learn to appreciate the rituals and values of a particular sport and they can begin to understand the beauty and meaning of a well-played game. By participating in fairly graded competitions, students have the opportunity to learn the value of perseverance, the satisfaction of improvement, and the fulfillment that comes from contributing to a team effort and having that contribution recognized. None of these lessons accrue automatically; teachers and students have to work together to ensure that these outcomes prevail.

Fair Play As the Central Focus for Behavior Development

Our approach to behavior development is grounded in the concept of fair play. We choose this approach because fair play is recognized throughout the sporting world as the central concept for social development in children's and youth sport. **Fair play** has a much broader meaning than just playing by the rules. It also includes respect for others, always participating with the right spirit and attitude, valuing equal opportunity, and behaving responsibly as a teammate and player. Most national sport organizations and many local community sport organizations have fair play programs and fair play codes of conduct. Using fair play as the central focus of social and behavior development in Sport Education should enable an easier and more complete transfer of the attitudes and behaviors of fair play from one setting to another.

The **goals of the fair play** focus in Sport Education are as follows.

- Participate fully and responsibly. Be on time. Be responsible in fulfilling your team and class tasks. Participate with enthusiasm.
- Give your best effort. Sport competition is most meaningful when all competitors give a full effort. Teams develop best when all teammates make a good effort in all their roles. Sport Education works best for all students when referees, scorekeepers, duty teams, coaches, and managers give a good effort and cooperate with each other.
- Respect the rights and feelings of teammates and opponents. Students should maintain self-control and respect and value everyone's right to participate fully and fairly in practices and competitions. When conflicts arise, students should respect and value ways to resolve those conflicts peacefully.
- Be a good sport. Play hard and play by the rules. Respect those who enforce the rules. Appreciate the effort of teammates and opponents. Be graceful in victory and dignified in defeat.
- Be helpful and not harmful. Look for ways to help your teammates, classmates, and teacher. Avoid putting down others or bullying. Express appreciation to good play and tasks well done.

Depending on the age and experience of your students, you will articulate and explain these fair play goals differently. While in one sense the goals do represent somewhat of a progression, this does not mean that you focus first on participating fully and responsibly and then proceed to another goal. Goals will have to be revisited continually to ensure that students not only learn and internalize the actions and behaviors that specifically relate to that goal but also come to value those behaviors and why they are important.

> **W**e could all put our ideas forward on what to do in the practices and discussed what went wrong in the games and worked out how to help each other to improve our game. It was good for people to learn about the team situation and pick up volleyball skills as well.
>
> —Tenth grade student, New Zealand

   Sport Education provides the context in which these fair play goals can be achieved. The affiliation of students with teams and the multiple roles students have to fulfill for a season to be successful create endless opportunities for teachers to emphasize fair play goals and for students to learn what it means to achieve the goals. Teams have regular meetings in which they make decisions together. Teams compete in ways that count toward a seasonal championship. Because all members of a team must contribute for the team to be successful, situations are created where more-skilled and less-skilled teammates must interact and support one another. Students refereeing contests and keeping score are put in situations where they make judgments and decisions, to which competitors react. All of these situations have the potential to create tension, disagreement, and even confrontation. It is within these contexts that students have the opportunity to grow in their **personal and social responsibility.** To think that students will learn the fair play qualities without these opportunities is to make fair play an academic exercise only, as if fair play could be taught by having students read about fair play and identify the qualities correctly on a written test.

> **I** think the benefits were that the kids themselves could see how far they had come from their beginning stage . . . they saw their development . . . it built their confidence because their team around them all the time were saying, "Oh, don't worry" . . . the lower-skilled players, even when they made mistakes, they were supported, they weren't hammered.
>
> —High school teacher, Australia

Teaching Fair Play

Strategies for teaching fair play will differ depending on the age and experience of students. The overall strategy is to make fair play an important, integral, and pervasive part of all that is done in Sport Education. You can accomplish this task using the following tools:

   • *Use codes of conduct.* Codes of conduct are specific descriptions of dimensions of behavior that define a particular role. Teachers should develop an overall **code of conduct** for the class that emphasizes the fair play goals described earlier (see figure 7.1 and the accompanying CD-ROM). Codes of conduct that emphasize the difference between fair play and unfair play are often helpful (see table 7.1). You should develop specific codes of conduct for coaches and referees also. (We

Sport Education Fair Play Code of Conduct

To ensure quality practice and good contests and games all players should do the following:

Participate fully and responsibly.

- Be on time.
- Do your part in team and class tasks.
- Participate enthusiastically.

Give your best effort.

- Try hard when practicing and playing.
- Try hard at your duty team roles.
- Cooperate with teammates in all roles.

Show respect to teammates and opponents.

- Always control your own behavior.
- Support everyone's right to participate fully.
- Try to resolve conflicts peacefully and quickly.
- Support your team and teammates in all ways.

Be a good sport.

- Play by the rules and give it your best at all times.
- Respect the referees.
- Show appreciation for teammates and opponents.
- Be a good sport in both winning and losing situations.

Be helpful and not harmful.

- Look for ways to be supportive of teammates.
- Avoid putting down others.
- Be willing to be a positive influence when you see put-downs or bullying.
- Always show your appreciation for good play and hard work.

Figure 7.1   Sample sport education fair play code of conduct.

Fair Play Resources

gratefully acknowledge the influence of Don Hellison's work on our approaches to the fair play system.)

   • *Use fair play contracts.* Many teachers have success using contracts. Students are asked to read, discuss, and sign the contract prior to competitions (see figure 7.2). All students could sign such a player **fair play contract** at the start of a season. Again, some teachers have had good success with codes of conduct that show the differences between fair and unfair players (see table 7.1). Contracts for coaches and referees would use more expectations for fair play that are specific to those roles. Figures 7.3 and 7.4 show contracts for coaches and officials from the New Zealand national fair play program. You can find examples of codes of conduct and contracts on the accompanying CD-ROM.

Table 7.1 Fair Player and Unfair Player Characteristics

Fair player characteristics	Unfair player characteristics
Follows rules	Criticizes play of others
Accepts officials' calls	Yells at officials
Compliments good play of others	Blames mistakes on others
Encourages teammates	Bosses other players
Plays own position	Hogs space and dominates play
Helps less-skilled classmates	Makes fun of less-skilled classmates
Is gracious in victory and defeat	Gloats in victory, sulks in defeat
Tries hard to apply skills	Will not work unless at center of play
Plays under control	Loses temper frequently
Wants everybody to play and succeed	Favors only a few classmates
Plays hard but fair	Tries to use rules to gain advantage

Reprinted, by permission, from P. Griffin and J. Placek, 1983, *Fair play in the gym: Race and sex equity in physical education* (Amherst, MA: University of Massachusetts, Women's Equity Program), 132-133.

Fair Play Agreements for Students and Teacher

For the player

I, _____,

agree to

- always play by the rules,
- never argue with an official,
- remember that I am playing because I enjoy the sport,
- work at achieving my personal best,
- show appreciation for good plays and good players,
- control my temper and not be a show-off, and
- play fairly at all times.

_____
Signature

_____
Date

For the teacher

I, _____,

agree to

- remember that students play for fun,
- encourage my students and offer constructive criticism,
- instruct my students to follow both the letter and the spirit of the rules,
- teach students that officials are important parts of the game,
- encourage my students to be good sports,
- give every participant a chance to play and to learn the skills, and
- remember that my actions speak louder than my words.

_____
Signature

_____
Date

Figure 7.2 Sample fair play agreement for students and teacher.

Source: "Fair Play–It's Your Call!: A Resource Manual for Coaches" (p.25) by Fair Play Canada. Copyright 1994 by Canadian Centre for Ethics in Sport.

The Fair Play Promise for [X Organization's] Coaches

Good sport is about positive attitude. As a coach you set the standards. Play your part to help make each game a success—play fairly.

To the best of my ability I will do the following:

- Set personal behavior standards for myself and those I coach to follow
- Give each player the same amount of my attention and time
- Provide every player with the same opportunities to play the game
- Never argue with the referee, encourage cheating, or make excuses for losing
- Always be positive and never shout at or ridicule players
- Respect players' efforts regardless of whether we have won or lost
- Encourage respect for the opposition and officials
- Keep winning and losing in perspective with personal challenge and enjoyment
- Give it my all and not get ugly

Signed: _____

Always give it your all but don't get ugly

Figure 7.3 Sample fair play contract for coaches.

Adapted, by permission, from SPARC, New Zealand.

Fair Play Contract for Referees

Good sport is about positive attitude. You can set the right tone and help make the game a success. Play your part—play fairly.

To the best of my ability I will do the following:

- Control the game in a fair and positive manner
- Be consistent and fair in my decisions
- Help players understand rules by explaining decisions where appropriate
- Do what I can to make sure players enjoy the game
- Encourage fair play and not tolerate foul play of any kind
- Always be firm and friendly

Signed: _____

Figure 7.4 Sample fair play contract for referees.

Adapted, by permission, from SPARC, New Zealand.

• *Use posters and messages.* The expectations for fair play have to be made constantly and pervasively present in physical education spaces and in communications. You should display a **fair play poster** that lists the basic expectations and refer to it continually. The fair play expectations on the poster do not have to include all the details articulated in the fair play goals just described. Instead, choose descriptive, age-appropriate phrases that signify the larger concepts embodied in the phrase. The fair play code shown in figure 7.5 was developed by the Commission for Fair Play in Canada (n.d.). Notice that it also has a fair play slogan: Good sports make good sport. The slogan can be particularly helpful with younger students. In New Zealand's current fair play campaign, the slogan is: Always give it heaps but don't get ugly.

• *Conduct awareness talks.* Students should regularly have the opportunity to discuss issues of fair play. Awareness talks (Hellison, 1996) can occur with individual teams, during closure at the end of class, or at any teachable moment within a class. Awareness talks often work best when they are precipitated by specific incidents in class. Awareness talks should not only occur after an example of unfair play; you should recognize instances of fair play that are exemplary of the code of conduct and discuss them with students.

• *Develop procedures for dealing with inappropriate behavior.* You (alone or with students) should develop specific procedures for dealing with inappropriate behavior such as violations of class management rules or violations of the fair play code of conduct. Many teachers have success with procedures that include a progression of consequences, from the least severe to the most severe. These consequences may include a reprimand, loss of fair play points, time out, and loss of privileges, among others. It is helpful if you display these consequences for inappropriate behavior prominently in the gymnasium, preferably near the code of conduct poster.

• *Develop procedures for resolving conflicts.* Sport Education is successful in engaging students fully. When students really care about their season, it is inevitable that conflicts will arise. Disputes within teams will occur when they have to decide which members will play in particular brackets of a competition. Disputes between referees and players will occur. With young students many teachers have had success with simple strategies to resolve minor disputes—strategies such as odds and evens or paper, scissors, rocks. The routine then becomes that minor disputes are quickly decided through the appointed mechanism and players return to action immediately with no further argument. In Australia and New Zealand, especially at the high school level, teachers typically form a dispute panel. The

Fair Play Code of Conduct

Respect the rules.

Respect the officials and their decisions.

Respect your opponent.

Give everybody an equal chance to participate.

Maintain your self-control at all times.

Good sports make good sport.

Figure 7.5 Sample fair play code of conduct.

Reference: From Commission for Fair Play for Kids: A Handbook of Activities for Teaching Fair Play. Copyright 1994 by the Canadian Centre for Ethics in Sport.

panel meets to make decisions about disputes, undesirable conduct (e.g., non-participation, seriously unfair play, and so forth), and disagreements about the fairness of a competition. The teacher is frequently a member of the panel, which decides the issue and suggests a remedy.

• *Include fair play in the championship point system.* Many Sport Education models have a point system that determines the championship. Teams get points for wins, practicing well, doing out-of-class work, and the like. Many teachers have teams start the season with a certain number of fair play points. Points are then deducted from the team's total when team members behave in ways that violate the behavior expectations emphasized in the fair play code.

• *Use multiple ways of recognizing fair play.* You should recognize instances of fair play as they occur, much as you would recognize a good tactical play in a team game or a good individual technique performance. You should recognize fair play during closure of class. Often teachers use season awards for fair play. Students can have homework assignments that emphasize fair play, such as creating murals or poster designs for fair play. You should devote a section of the bulletin board to fair play. You can use small stars with players' names that have shown fair play, a fair play player of the season award, and the like.

10
Awards/Fair Play Awards

14
Chapter Slides

CREATING AND SUSTAINING ENERGY IN SPORT EDUCATION

The goals of effective class management and development of personal and social responsibility through a fair play system are complementary. Teachers have frequently reported that their experiences with Sport Education have allowed them to achieve goals they had been frustrated in achieving for years and freed them to become the kind of teacher they most want to be. It is amazing how an energized and increasingly self-directed class of students can change how a teacher views his or her work.

> *I feel I'm not personally teaching skills to the same depth, but it is debatable whether this really matters since the quality of the games by the end of the season is far and way above that which I would normally get them to.*
>
> —High school teacher, Australia

The class management suggestions in this chapter are meant to allow Sport Education lessons to flow smoothly and to have an energized pace. For more than a quarter of a century, research has shown that lessons that run smoothly and at a brisk pace not only accomplish more outcomes but also have fewer behavior disruptions (Kounin, 1970; Doyle, 1986, Siedentop & Tannehill, 2000). A lesson that has momentum has no breaks, no times when activities or transitions slow down or come to a halt. A smooth, well-paced lesson is one in which segments of the lesson flow quickly from one to another. It all begins with the entry routines in which class begins promptly with a well-paced activity. The many transitions within a lesson occur rapidly without disruption. Teachers have specific methods for dealing with unpredictable intrusions, such as a note from the principal, a public address announcement, or an injured student.

Effective sport educators also make clear that they convey their expectations for a smooth, briskly-paced class to their students. They publicly and privately recognize and praise students who are contributing to these goals. Teachers also show enthusiasm for the season, the particular lesson, and for the students themselves. Together, the establishment of routines and the focus on producing an energized class atmosphere will eventually create a norm for the class.

The fair play suggestions in this chapter are intended to provide a method for helping students to become responsible, independent learners who also show respect and concern for their classmates and for the activities in which they are participating. This kind of energy is different from the energy just described, but just as important to the success of Sport Education in the long run. You should not forget that a long-term goal of Sport Education is for students to become enthusiastic sportspersons. We expect that students who experience Sport Education for several years would develop both the skills and the predispositions to become involved in sport in the community, not only as participants, but also as coaches, referees, and in leadership roles. By first learning to care about the small sport culture in Sport Education in their own school physical education program, and by learning the important roles that sustain that sport culture, they become equipped to participate in similar roles in sport cultures outside of school, whether a community sport program, a youth sport league, or a sport club.

SUPPORTING AND CELEBRATING MANAGEMENT AND BEHAVIOR DEVELOPMENT

14
Chapter Slides

It is important that teachers both support and celebrate students when they manage themselves well and when they begin to show the behaviors associated with fair play. You can do this in a number of ways. You should frequently provide consistent feedback on performance, recognize improvement, and point out particularly good examples of both performance and improvement. It is also easy to include duty team performance as an element in the point system, so when teams perform well in their duty roles they can also gain in the standings. As indicated earlier, you can also incorporate fair play points for teams into the point system. All of these strategies should become part of making the season festive for the students and helping to develop the class as a learning community.

Management and fair play recognition and awards should be a prominent part of the culminating activity that celebrates the end of each season. Teachers have created **awards for good duty team performance.** You can include **awards for coaches and managers** who fulfill contracts. Fair play awards of all kinds are appropriate, both for team and individual recognition. The accompanying CD-ROM contains many examples of awards that you can use or modify for local purposes.

10
Awards

Good class management and positive behavior development are crucial elements of the Sport Education model. In a real sense, they provide the foundation for all else that is achieved in the way of sport-specific outcomes and personal development outcomes such as leadership. We have tried in this chapter to provide specific strategies for achieving these goals.

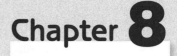

Chapter **8**

Designing the Season to Accomplish Goals

The Sport Education season is longer than a traditional physical education unit. Each season has a strong focus on teaching techniques and tactics, and organizing a series of competitions that allow students to improve, all leading to a culminating event that ends the season in a festive atmosphere. This chapter outlines and explains concerns that must be addressed when planning a Sport Education season. Throughout the chapter, we will make references to other key chapters that have contributed to your understanding of the Sport Education model, especially chapters 3 through 7, which are pertinent to designing a season that you will use in your own program.

14

Chapter Slides

LOCAL CONSIDERATIONS

14

Chapter Slides

You will always have local factors to consider when designing a Sport Education season. No single design format will be equally useful in elementary, middle, and high school settings. Local considerations that most dramatically affect the design of a season are the amount of time allocated for physical education, the number of students in each class, the nature of the facility space, and the type and amount of equipment available. At many Sport Education presentations, we have been asked, "What features of the model are most important and must be adhered to?" Our first answer is always, "The amount of time devoted to a season." At the elementary level we have seen good Sport Education seasons done over 10 to 12 class periods lasting at least 40 minutes each. The standard amount of time at high school seems to be 20 class sessions lasting at least 45 minutes each, but we have seen good examples of seasons that are longer. We think these time allotments are adequate. As you will see in this chapter, however, if you try to do the Sport Education model in very short seasons, you simply will not have enough time to achieve your goals.

I think it's better to learn one thing and learn it well, than learn a whole lot of different things and skip over all the things you need to know. We were learning just how to do it . . . we never got to play a game against someone else to see how good we were. It was good to see where we were placed and if we could improve . . . become better.

—High school student, New Zealand

Local constraints that can be accommodated fairly easily are the number of students in each class, the nature of the facility, and the amount of equipment available. These constraints exert their primary influence on the choice of activity for the season. If you have large classes, then small-sided sector games such as softball can easily accommodate 40 to 50 students with modest numbers of balls and bats and can be done on any grassy school ground. You can organize 3v3 volleyball in most gymnasiums with homemade nets and balls that, while not regulation, are perfectly useful for volleyball. To do an Olympic gymnastics Sport Education season with a class of 40 would require a special facility with abundant equipment, but you can do acrosport and rhythmic gymnastics without specialized equipment and spaces. Invasion games such as ultimate Frisbee and team handball can be done inside or outside and require very little in terms of specialized equipment. Thus, while these factors may constrain the choice of a seasonal activity, they should not prevent you from using the Sport Education model.

Chapter Slides

DEFINING OUTCOMES

Once you have chosen a sport or activity, the most crucial step in the design process is defining outcomes. An outcome is a description of what a student will know and be able to do as a result of participation during the season (Siedentop & Tannehill, 2000). In Sport Education, we try to define authentic outcomes (Wiggins, 1993). Sport Education outcomes are authentic if they specify techniques, tactics, and knowledge that will be demonstrated in the context of doing the activity.

For example, consider how to think about the outcome of skillful passing in basketball. In a basketball season, students should learn how to recognize an open teammate who is in a position of advantage relative to defenders and deliver the ball to the teammate quickly with the appropriate pass (bounce pass, chest pass, and so on). This outcome requires a combination of tactical awareness (location of the open teammate who is at most advantage), technique (chest pass, bounce pass, and so on), and skill (as defined in chapter 2). Thinking about the outcome of passing in this way will help you to design practice activities that will likely lead to increased proficiency in passing. While having students stand some distance from each other and practice different passes might be a starting point, it clearly is just that and nothing more. To develop the techniques and tactics associated with improved passing, you will have to create practice situations that are dynamic and gamelike. For example, begin with simple, modified games that have fewer players and are less complex, but which allow for students to master beginning techniques and tactics, such as 2v1 or 3v2 basketball drills or games that emphasize moving to positions of advantage and executing passes.

If you want to or are required to do formal assessments, thinking about the authentic outcome will make it immediately clear how you will need to assess passing. Having students stand 15 feet from a wall and counting the number of chest passes they make in 30 seconds is not an authentic assessment of passing skills. On the other hand, you could use the concept of assists as one authentic proxy measure for passing proficiency, because it is a common statistic kept in most basketball games. The point is that you must assess authentic outcomes in gamelike performance settings. In the authentic assessment literature, important opportunities for assessing outcomes are often referred to as exhibitions (that is, games, meets, and performances).

. . . we speak of such a final challenge as an exhibition. It is a "test" in the sense that the big game is a "test." Unlike the conventional "final," the exhibition—piano recital or a play—lets a performer show off or "exhibit" what he or she knows. (Wiggins, 1987, p. 15)

The culminating event in Sport Education is clearly an exhibition in this sense—such as a championship game, gymnastics routine, folk dance, or race—and a performance in that event is a key part of seasonal assessment. All Sport Education competitions, from the first in a season to the culminating event, are exhibitions that lend themselves to authentic assessment.

The design process, therefore, begins with identifying a limited set of authentic outcomes that you want students to achieve in a season. Outcomes should be considered not only for techniques and tactics, but also for the knowledge and techniques that students will have to demonstrate in Sport Education roles, such as referee and scorekeeper. We urge you to consider a limited set of outcomes. When educators begin to think about developing a curriculum around authentic outcomes, they often keep in mind a slogan that has become central to that approach to education: less is more. The fact is that too many units of instruction are best described as a mile wide and an inch deep. If you try to stuff too many outcomes into a season, you will likely be disappointed in the results.

KEY FEATURES FOR DESIGNING A SUCCESSFUL SEASON

14
Chapter Slides

As we just indicated, the first step is to decide on a limited set of outcomes to be achieved. What level of skill (techniques + tactics = skill) these outcomes represent will depend a great deal on the experiences and levels of tactical awareness and technical competence that students bring to the season. It will also depend on the activity you choose, in the sense that if an activity that is new to most students (e.g., cricket or team handball) it will require more time to master the basic techniques and tactics for beginning play. If the students have widely varying degrees of previous experience, then you will have to develop some parallel outcomes for students with less and more experience. In most schools teachers designing a soccer season at the eighth grade level will have some students who have played several years of youth soccer and others who have never competed in soccer. In such cases, you should plan graded competitions with games modified differently for those who are less and more experienced. For example, if you choose the three-teams-a-class model used so frequently in Sport Education, then

*E*valuation of the 1993 SE I project concluded that teachers were genuinely surprised by the outcomes they were experiencing using the Sport Education model with their students. Participation levels were up, skill levels were up, students were learning to umpire, coach and manage more effectively and in many cases the students were organising their own learning environment.

—Report for the Sport Education II Project, SPARC

you should assign students with different levels of experience to different teams so that A and B levels of competition can be arranged with games modified differently for the students with less and more experience. The B level for students with the least experience might be a 3v3 competition on a smaller field with simpler rules, while the A level might be 5v5 competition on a larger field with rules closer to regulation soccer. Results from each of these competitions would count equally toward the seasonal championship.

When designing your season, we suggest you take the following steps (Siedentop & Tannehill, 2000).

1. *Develop a limited set of authentic outcomes.* If you are designing a basketball unit, do not assume that students have to learn both zone and person-to-person defenses. Pick one kind of defense and a fairly simple offensive pattern to teach to students, especially if they have had limited basketball experiences. If you are designing a folk dance season, choose a limited set of dances that progress from less to more complex in terms of the steps required, and give students time to learn to perform each dance well.

2. *Design down from those outcomes.* Start from the level of performance you expect students to show in the culminating event. Then, given the number of days allocated to the season, back down gradually to see where you will start with technical, tactical, and knowledge instruction and practice. This exercise will help you to be conservative in your ambitions for how you expect students to perform at the end of the season. As Launder (2001, p. 67) has so cogently suggested: "The critical issue here—and one that is rarely addressed—is the amount of training or practice time necessary to achieve worthwhile improvement in the specific components of effective play." Ask yourself these questions: What techniques will students have to acquire? What tactics will they have to learn? How much time will they need to feel comfortable and perform well in activities and games designed to lead to the culminating event? What kinds of activities and modified games will help students to progress toward the intended outcomes? Having answered these questions, you can then realistically assess the potential answers to the following three questions from Launder: What must be covered if outcomes are to be achieved? What should be covered if good use is made of available time? What might be covered if time permits?

3. *Plan for and check alignment of various steps towards the outcomes.* Alignment exists when instruction, practice activities, and competitions lead to the desired outcomes. Because Sport Education outcomes are defined in terms of ability to perform well in games, contests, and activities, the instruction and practice should clearly lead toward that goal. You should design technique practice activities so that they are similar to how the techniques are used in competition. Tactical awareness should grow sequentially through a series of activities that introduce the major tactical issues of a game or contest and then gradually become more complex as students gain more awareness of the primary attacking and defending options as play unfolds.

4. *Carefully consider the distribution of sequenced experiences.* Experiences in a season should all contribute to the outcomes desired for the season. As mentioned earlier, outcomes should be limited; that is, students do not need to learn everything there is to learn about the sport or activity that is the focus for the season. Likewise, not every class has to contribute to fitness, knowledge, technique, tactical, and social goals. If fitness is done, it should be specific to the sport or activity that is the focus for the season. Evidence exists that students in Sport Education

are typically quite active during classes, especially in classes of teachers that have developed the kinds of management routines described in chapter 7, so the needs for moderate to vigorous physical activity are usually filled quite well during the season. We have continuously argued for an approach that sequences competitions that lead to seasonal outcomes. The elementary soccer example on pages 63-64 is one good example. Another might be in a basketball season in which the first competition is 2v2 with the pick and roll as the primary tactical focus for attacking. Students would need to learn to dribble, set screens, roll from the screens, and pass. Defenders would need to learn to anticipate screens, switch on signal, and recover to defend a different player. Students should learn these tactics and techniques, then apply them in a 2v2 half-court competition that counts toward the seasonal championship. When this competition is completed, a 3v3 game could be introduced with teams using person-to-person defense. Teams could learn a pass and screen-away offense, for which they would be able to transfer the learning outcomes achieved in the first competition to this slightly more complex game. The major tactical additions would be floor balance, off-the-ball support, help-side defense, back-door cutting, and the like.

PREPARING FOR THE SEASON

Chapter Slides

This section describes the items that you will need to think about and prepare for prior to the start of the season (see table 8.1). We assume that you have developed basic class management routines (see chapter 7) and would use these routines throughout the school year for all the Sport Education seasons, so we do not address most of them here, other than those that likely change for each season. We also assume that a fair play system has been developed and will be in use for each season (see the extensive description of the fair play approach to behavior development described in chapter 7). The accompanying CD-ROM also includes season **planning worksheets** to assist in the season preparations.

Planning Worksheets

Table 8.1 Preparation Needed Before the Start of the Season

Task	Description
Selection of sport or activity	Decide on a sport or activity and how to modify it. Identify the sequence of competitions and specify rules for each.
Space and equipment	Know court or field layouts for each competition. Know equipment needed for each competition.
Length of season	Know number of days/season and hours/day to gauge total time to allocate to various elements of the season.
Teams	Decide on number of teams, method of selection, and materials needed, if any, for selection process.
Roles	Most likely: Player, referee, scorekeeper, coach, manager, and fitness leader Optional: Statistician, publicity director
Support for learning roles	Create duty sheets, expectations, contracts, and so on.
Team identity	Choose nickname, team color, mascot, team cheer, team space on bulletin board.

(continued)

Table 8.1   *(continued)*

Task	Description
Duty team responsibilities	Equipment to appropriate venue, referee, and scorekeeper at each venue
Duty team equipment needs	Scoresheets, whistles, clipboards, balls, referee pinnies
Class routines for this season	Home field, entry activity
Content development	Game modifications and sequences, teaching of techniques and tactics, teaching of rules, refereeing, and scorekeeping; sequence of learning activities
Instructional support	Critical elements and common errors of techniques to be taught; support for learning tactical concepts; posters, handouts, and so on
Entry activity	Technique, stretching, or fitness focus? Prepare daily technique or fitness posters.
Fair play	What components of the fair play system to emphasize? How will they be assessed?
Culminating event	Decide on the nature of the event. One day or multiple class sessions? Prepare awards.
Assessment protocols	Decide how performance of roles will be assessed. Create assessment protocol for game play in addition to data from scorekeepers.
Seasonal championship	Identify all activities that contribute to earning points toward the championship—fair play, duty team, roles, wins, and so on. Identify point values that are appropriate to each element. Create handout or poster so all students are aware of point system.

We need to reemphasize that a major feature of Sport Education is that the structure of the season is known at the outset. In most physical education classes, students often do not know what they will do when they enter the gym on any day, let alone what will they will be doing four weeks later. Successful Sport Education teachers typically prepare all materials prior to the season. Once students begin to experience Sport Education they will know what to expect and be able to assist in many ways.

A SEVENTH TO NINTH GRADE EXAMPLE

The following season might be appropriate for seventh, eighth, and ninth grades. With slight modifications you could use it for lower and higher grades. The context for the design is a physical education program that meets for three 50-minute periods each week. The design is planned for a coed class of 28 to 32 students, with a fairly even mix of boys and girls. The assumption is that the teacher has worked with these students before and has general knowledge of their skill levels. The particular school system has no interscholastic volleyball at this level. The gymnasium is standard size for a middle or junior high school. Nets with portable standards are available. Available are 12 regulation volleyballs and 12 volleyball trainer balls that are softer and slightly larger than regulation. This example assumes that this is not the first time students have participated in the Sport Education model.

Outcomes should be identified for techniques, tactics, student roles necessary for the season, and rules that will govern the various competitions comprising the season. We do not suggest that this has to be a formal exercise in identification but rather that teachers think about the level of performance they would expect to develop given their knowledge of where their students will be at the start of the season and where they would expect them to be at the end of the season. Doing this allows teachers to identify the instruction they will have to provide and the practice activities that will help students to improve in the techniques, tactics, and roles that are identified.

Outcomes

Students will demonstrate appropriate techniques and tactics in 2v2, 3v3, and 4v4 volleyball games.

- Techniques: passing, setting, spiking, dinking, blocking, and digging
- Tactics: directing the ball through passing and setting, reading defense to spike or dink, redirecting balls to angles of advantage, off-the-ball support, maintaining spacing, moving from attack to defend and vice versa
- Refereeing and scorekeeping: calling net violations, out of bounds, and held balls; keeping team score of points, blocks, and spikes or dinks that lead to points
- Rules: held ball, out of bounds, net violations, rally scoring

Decisions Made Prior to the Start of the Season

- Sport: volleyball; 2v2, 3v3, and 4v4 competitions, free ball to start each rally, rally scoring, nets lower than regulation, court spaces for each competition small enough to allow players to cover space if they move appropriately
- Space: gymnasium; configure courts of different sizes for different competitions
- Equipment: 12 regulation volleyballs, 12 volleyball trainer balls
- Length of season: 20 days, 50-minute class sessions
- Teams: 3 teams, 9 to 11 players a team, coaches chosen first, coaches assist in creating evenly matched teams, coaches assigned to teams through blind draw, teams to choose name, colors, and mascot; teams develop a cheer for before and after competitions
- Roles: player, coach, manager, referee, scorekeeper, fitness leader, statistician
- Duty team: manage equipment, organize players to venues, referee, keep score
- Home courts: teams assigned to specific net spaces for warm-ups and practices, each with 8 balls available
- Content development: passing and setting learned together, spiking and dinking learned together, blocking learned in isolation then combined with spiking and dinking; control and redirection of ball emphasized in all passing and setting activities; reading defense emphasized in all spiking and dinking activities; floor balance and changing from attacking to defending emphasized throughout
- Instructional support: posters describing critical elements and common errors for all techniques posted on gymnasium walls

- Entry activity: practicing techniques in gamelike drills; drills for day posted on bleachers
- Culminating event: 4v4 coed tournament with A and B levels; final games videotaped
- Awards: overall seasonal team champion and runner-up; A- and B-level champions and runners-up from 2v2, 3v3, and 4v4 competitions; best fair play team; best duty team; best team mascot and cheer; most improved team; coach recognition; manager recognition; videotape of championship 4v4 games shown on final day along with awards

Sample Season Block Plans

DAILY SCHEDULE

In chapter 7, we explained a number of class routines that are important to efficient use of time in Sport Education. Use of these routines will help to ensure that the time you plan for learning, practice, and competition is used for those purposes. Daily lessons in Sport Education fall into three categories: (1) learning and practice days, (2) practice and competition days, and (3) competition days. Each of these days will have a slightly different rhythm. Each begins with an entry routine that is either fitness or technique focused or some combination of the two. You should make sure that teams have some time to plan strategy and placement of members in various competitions that await them. Learning and practice days will typically include both guided and independent practice (see chapter 2). The guided practice is typically teacher-led with a direct instruction format. The independent practice is typically done by teams in their home spaces, with coaches taking a lead role and the teacher moving throughout the entire space to assist. The practice tasks assigned should be as gamelike as possible, and teammates should be encouraged to help one another. Practices should become as routine as possible. You can use drills that offer students the chance to practice the relevant techniques in gamelike configurations throughout the season.

Days that include both practice and competition typically rely on practice tasks that students have learned and know how to do without teacher explanations and prompting; that is, they have become practice routines, with the emphasis on technique refinement and increased tactical awareness. Competitions may be scrimmages or they may count toward the seasonal championship. Time should be allotted for teams to plan for that day's competition and to make any changes necessary because of absences. At the appropriate time in the lesson, the teacher signals the start of the competition phase and the duty team for the first round of games quickly organizes the referees, scorekeepers, and equipment. Because competitions are timed, all the volleyball games will start and stop at the same time. Part of the referee's job is to keep the game moving forward at a brisk pace. A specific time is allotted between games for the next duty team to prepare for the next game and for team managers to get the right players to the appropriate courts.

Competition days will occur at any point in a competition schedule, not just at the end of the season. Each new competition will be a slightly more complex activity, and students will need time to learn and practice the techniques and tactics needed for the new competition. At the start of any new competition phase, teams will need time to work out team assignments for both competition and duty team roles.

Lessons should end with a closure period in which teachers comment on the day's activities, and exemplary performance in practice and duty team duties and competition can be recognized. Students and teams who showed good fair play behaviors should also be recognized. Next in this chapter we will provide a series of snapshots of daily lessons in various activities. Table 8.2 shows a daily schedule for the volleyball season.

Table 8.2 Volleyball Season Daily Schedule

Day	Focus
1	Introduction of volleyball, appointment or selection of coaches, guided and independent practice of passing and setting with tactical focus of control and redirection, guided and independent practice of spiking and dinking with focus on reading defense, description of home courts and entry routine, description of seasonal schedule of competitions, net and heldball rules introduced. Coaches meet with teacher to place students on teams to create fair competition.
2	Teams announced and coaches assigned to teams, refresher points on techniques learned, practice drills by teams in home courts, guided and independent practice for blocking, 2v2 game introduced with freeball start to each rally, rally scoring introduced, team practice at home court in 2v2 format. Duty team responsibilities introduced. Teams to choose name, colors, mascot, and team cheer.
3	Practice drills in home courts, refereeing and scorekeeping introduced with whole class demonstration, 2v2 team practice in home courts with practice of refereeing and scorekeeping, teams begin to form pairings for first competition. The A competition will be girls, B competition boys, and C competition coed.
4	Practice drills in home courts, whole class session with focus on tactics (spacing, court coverage, looking for angles, switching from attack to defend and vice versa), team practice in home courts. Teams perform their cheer and show their chosen mascot.
5	Practice drills in home courts, 2v2 scrimmage day, team rotation and duty team assignments, brief feedback session after each timed game and rotation to next game with focus on managing the competition to ensure that everybody has full time to play. 8-min games, 6 courts, girls, boys, and coed teams from each of the 3 teams, 3 games/game session with a total of 9 games; substitutions on the fly at 3 and 6 min **Game session** / **Teams** / **Duty team** 1 / 1v2 / 3 2 / 1v3 / 2 3 / 2v3 / 1
6	Practice drills in home courts, whole class review of scrimmage-day play with focus on technique and tactics. Review of refereeing and scorekeeping issues raised from scrimmage. Team practice on 2v2 tactics and to determine final placement of players on girl's, boy's, and coed teams for the 2v2 competition.
7	Practice drills in home courts. 2v2 competition day. Same game pattern as on day 5. Games are 12 min long with substitutions at 4 and 8 min.
8	Practice drills in home courts. 2v2 competition day 2. Same game pattern. Team rosters can be adjusted. 2v2 championship determined by won–loss record in the 4 games played. Tiebreaker by points scored. Announcement of champion and runner-up. Team statisticians meet to arrange to post total statistics next day.
9	Practice drills in home courts. Whole class review of 2v2 competition. Whole class guided practice on 3v3 competition tactics with court coverage, angles, and transitions from attacking to defending. Teams to identify players for setter and hitter positions. New practice drill with setter position shown. Court size and net height for 3v3 competition reviewed. Independent 3v3 practice by teams in home courts.

(continued)

Table 8.2   (continued)

Day	Focus
10	Practice drills in home courts. Teams continue 3v3 practice for the boys' and girls' team competitions. In last 20 min teams can informally practice against other teams.
11	Practice drills in home courts. 3v3 scrimmage day. Team rotation and duty team assignments same as on day 5. Girl's competition and boy's competition. Games are 12-min duration with substitutions at 4 and 8 min. Each new point starts with free ball. Rally scoring. Closure to review issues raised during competition related to tactics, techniques, refereeing, or scorekeeping.
12	Practice drills in home courts. First 3v3 competition day. Team rotation and duty team assignments the same as for scrimmage day. Game format the same. Closure with teacher-led review of today's games.
13	Same as day 12. Closure with coaches-led review of today's games.
14	Same as day 13. Champion and runner-up determined. Statisticians meet to organize 3v3 statistics to post next class period.
15	Practice drills in home courts. Class views video of men's and women's elite level 6v6 volleyball. Teacher describes where volleyball is played in local community and what organizations support volleyball. Video of beach VB competition is shown. Students discuss differences in the two forms of VB.
16	Practice drills in home courts. Whole class description of 4v4 coed volleyball. Teams to identify setters and hitters (one hitter must be a girl). Teams practice 4v4 at home courts. Each team will field a coed A team and a coed B team.
17	Practice drills in home courts. 4v4 scrimmage day in A and B competitions. Same format as in day 5, except 2 games/session rather than 3. Closure to review performance and answer questions.
18	Practice drills in home courts. 4v4 competition day. Same format as day 12.
19	Practice drills in home courts. Round 2 of 4v4 competition.
20	Review video of 4v4 competition. Awards ceremony.

SAMPLE LESSONS

As mentioned earlier, three primary lesson types exist in Sport Education. The first type is learning and practice, which typically occur at the start of the season and also between competitions. The second lesson type is practice and competition. The competition can be a scrimmage or may count toward the seasonal championship. The third lesson type is a competition day. We do not suggest that Sport Education teachers do not teach during the days that reflect the second two types; they are always teaching as they work with teams and move about the space during team practices and competitions. It only means that during some days the primary structure of the lesson reflects time allocated to formal instruction that is typically whole-class focused.

Ninth Grade Badminton: Lesson Type 1

Class begins with students quickly organizing in their home courts, where they complete a brief stretching routine led by the fitness leader and then a clear drill that they have practiced each day. The class then gathers with their rackets at the common meeting space. The teacher leads a guided practice session on the drop shot. Critical elements and common errors are emphasized. Students mimic or shadow the appropriate movements for the drop shot. Questions are asked and answered. The teacher then demonstrates the drop shot drill that each team will practice. She also explains the drop shot challenge with which each team will end the session. Coaches are expected to be able to supervise this drill. Students return to their home spaces where coaches quickly organize their teams into the drill. The teacher circulates, helping both players and coaches. The session culminates with the drop shot challenge. Team managers count the team scores. Class closure includes a review of the drop shot, recognition of the team scores, and review of fair play behavior for the day.

Sixth Grade Acrosport: Lesson Type 2

Class begins with students in their home spaces being led through the fitness and stretching routine by their fitness leader. On signal from the teacher, teams have several minutes to discuss the trios and quad routines they have been developing. Teams then practice the routines with emphasis on balance, poise, and style. On signal from the teacher, teams organize for practice competition that will not count toward the seasonal championship. The duty team for the first round organizes the space and become the judges for the competition. Three rounds of trio and quad routines are presented, with each team competing twice and serving as duty team once. A whole class closure focuses on reports from judges and teacher comments on the competitions.

Tenth Grade Tennis: Lesson Type 3

Class begins with teams reporting to their home courts and engaging in their practice warm-up routine that emphasizes various strokes. Team managers also are reminding teammates of the day's competition schedule and the format for play. After the entry practice period, the teacher gathers the students to remind them of key points in tactics and technique that need improvement based on her observations from the previous competition. Two rounds of competition will occur. On this day, the Williams Sisters team will compete against the Agassis team on courts 1 through 3. Courts 1 and 2 will be for singles and court 3 for doubles. On courts 4 through 6, the Davenports team will compete against the Hewitts team using the same format. In Round 1, Courts 1 and 4 are first singles, courts 2 and 5 are second singles, and courts 3 and 6 are doubles. Games start with a serve from a line that is 6 feet in from the baseline. Noncompeting players from each team serve as umpires and ball retrievers. Games consist of each player having three service games. At the end of Round 1, players quickly reorganize for Round 2, which uses the identical format (third and fourth singles and second doubles). At the end of the second round, the class gathers for a review and recognition of good performances in play and in duty responsibilities.

Fifth Grade Orienteering: Lesson Type 2

Class begins with students completing a warm-up jog around the park space next to the school grounds. At the close of the warm-up jog, students gather in a central place where the teacher reviews the critical features of using a compass to determine a control point of direction. The teacher uses a questioning technique to make sure that students have the necessary understandings. Teams then gather in their home spaces and team managers get compasses ready while team coaches review the day's competition. The competition is a relay event in which runners from each team find a control point according to a specific compass reading they must make, then return to their teams with the next runner finding the subsequent control point. Students who have just finished a leg of the relay check their pulse rate immediately after crossing the finish line. Each team is responsible for recording their own times. For each phase of the relay, one team member acts as a reliability recorder for another team. At the end of the relay, teams calculate their total time and compare their own record with that of the record produced by the reliability recorder. Records are turned over to team statisticians, who will update the seasonal record charts by the next class meeting. During closure, the teacher and students discuss problems encountered and pulse rates observed.

Eleventh Grade Weight Training: Lesson Type 3

It is the first day of a three-day finale of the weight training season. Students in the five teams gather in their home spaces, where they are led in a warm-up and stretching period by their fitness leader. The day's competition will be two lifts and there are five weight categories each for boys and girls. When not competing, students occupy roles of scorekeeper, judge, recorder, or weight changer. The class sports board had decided that culminating competition to the season will consist of the bench press, leg press, lat pull-down, and biceps curls as exercises contested. In addition, an abdominal endurance test will be done. During today's competition session, the bench press and leg press will be contested by the two lightest weight categories, while the lat pull-down and the biceps curls will be contested by the middle weight categories. The highest weight category will see the championships of the abdominal endurance challenge, a popular event that is accompanied by considerable team support by the teammates of each competitor. During closure, the results are announced and the day one championship awards are presented.

Fourth Grade Soccer: Lesson Type 1

It is the first day of the second competition of the soccer season. In the initial phase of the season, students competed in simple 1v1 soccer games played on spaces and with rules similar to half-court basketball. In that early phase of the season, students learned the techniques of dribbling, shooting, tackling, and shielding. They also learned the concept of defensive space. The second competition will be 2v2 and in this first lesson of the second phase of the season, the teacher is introducing the techniques of passing and trapping, as well as tactical concepts of floor balance, off-the-ball support, centering, and cutting. Passing and trapping are introduced in a whole-class guided practice format. Students work in pairs (still in the whole class format) to begin to practice the techniques demonstrated. The teacher is able to see whether they have sufficient understanding to benefit from independent practice. The teacher also shows an initial drill that involves players working in pairs but continually moving rather than practicing the techniques from stationary positions. Teams then disperse to practice the drill in their home courts, with coaches taking an active role in helping their players learn the techniques. The teacher then gathers the students again and reviews strengths and weaknesses seen during the team practices. A 2v1 drill with one defender is introduced that begins to mimic the more dynamic play of a game. Teams then return to their home spaces to practice this drill. The teacher gathers the students for a closure that focuses on feedback on the techniques practiced and a further description of why they are so important in successful game play.

A NOTE FOR FIRST-TIME USERS

For teachers who want to try out the Sport Education model, we suggest that you do a bare bones version that requires less preparation and provides plenty of time to help students learn the routines and rhythms of a Sport Education season. In our experience with teachers who are first-time users, we have found the following suggestions to be useful.

- *Choose an activity with which you are familiar.* It will make it easy for you to plan for the technical and tactical content development. It will also make it easier for you to design modified games that help students learn the techniques and tactics as well as get abundant opportunities to practice.

- *Use only the basic student roles.* We suggest using the roles of coach, manager, fitness leader, referee, and scorekeeper.

- *Develop a simple fair play system.* You want students to cooperate, behave responsibly within their teams, and make a good effort. Using the suggestions in chapter 7, create a fair play system, explain it thoroughly to students, and provide constant reminders. We say this because in our experience, many students have not been accustomed to behaving responsibly in physical education without the constant supervision of the teacher.

- *Develop simple, modified games.* Keep rules to a minimum. Keep scorekeeping simple.

- *Devote more time to teaching the model as well as the content.* Students will have to learn about what is expected of coaches and managers, how teams will practice on their home courts, sometimes with teacher supervision. They will have to learn the duty team responsibilities and learn the importance of getting those responsibilities done quickly. This takes time and it is time well spent, so plan for it in your seasonal plan. Always remember that it is their first time, too.

> *I* am a referee so I am learning more about basketball. I feel better now when I am watching basketball because I can understand it better.
>
> —High school student, New Zealand

Keep the seasonal championship point system simple. Give points for the essential aspects of the season that will make it a success. We suggest that fair play points, competition points, and duty team points are the most important because it is student behavior in those areas that will make the season a success. For other roles, you might consider using **contracts** with recognition at the culminating event for having fulfilled the duties of coach and manager, two key roles in having teams function effectively. We also suggest that you check out the Frequently Asked Questions on the accompanying CD-ROM (Resource 12).

This chapter described in detail what happens during a Sport Education season. By understanding the kinds of activities that take place and the sequence of those activities across a season, you should have a much better sense of how to plan a season. It is obviously our judgment that teachers first trying the Sport

Education model should heed the recommendations presented in the section for first-time users. If you are a first-timer, it will take time for you and your students to become accustomed to the Sport Education model with its emphasis on student roles. Ample evidence shows, however, that when the second or third season rolls around, both students and teacher are much more comfortable with the model and are able to begin to stretch the model to its full potential.

Chapter 9

Assessment

14 Chapter Slides

In most schools, students in physical education receive a grade as they do in other subjects. In some schools, grades may only be in the form of a pass/fail or satisfactory/unsatisfactory report. Grading students always requires you to do some form of assessment. In some cases (far too often from our view), teachers grade students solely on attendance, dressing for class, and minimal involvement in activities, often referred to as show up, dress up, and stand up criteria for grading. However they are calculated, grades are a reality in most schools.

An increasing understanding exists among educators that assessment plays a key role in learning, and therefore has importance above and beyond grading. Assessment can be defined as the "variety of tasks and settings where students are given opportunities to demonstrate their knowledge, skill, understanding, and application of content in a context that allows continued learning and growth" (Siedentop & Tannehill, 2000, pp. 178-179). Assessment always requires some measurement, whether it be through tests, student work products such as essays or art work, performance records, or observation.

Assessment in physical education is not as easy as it is for classroom teachers. Because most outcomes in classroom subjects are cognitive, classroom teachers can assign homework, require essays, give quizzes, and give end-of-course exams. With these tools, they can create a series of permanent products that serve as performance indicators from which students get feedback about how they are doing and get to know their strengths and weaknesses. Teachers use some or all of these assessments to calculate grades. While physical education teachers can give quizzes and even require some written homework, the outcomes they are trying to achieve need to be assessed while students are performing physical techniques and tactics during class time; that is, the products in physical education classes are not permanent in the way that papers, quizzes, and exams are. Thus, someone must observe the performance and make a record of the performance evaluation. Many physical educators say that they simply do not have the time to do full assessments on all their students and still keep them actively involved in learning.

The Sport Education model presents many opportunities for assessment. It will allow you more opportunity to engage in and support assessment activities. The use of seasons (which are typically much longer than units) will create extended periods for you to evaluate student performance. The small group learning model and the emphasis on student responsibilities typically gets teachers out of the traffic director role, freeing them to spend more time observing students, providing feedback, and teaching. Many Sport Education teachers have noted that the model enables them to stand back and see the bigger picture of what is going on in their classes. Because Sport Education classes tend to be highly structured, with student coaches and managers occupying key roles in ensuring that activities move smoothly within the established structure, you will spend more of your time observing students perform—not only techniques and tactics, but also in their roles as referees, scorekeepers, managers, fitness leaders, and the like.

Using small-sided games, in which all students get equal opportunity to learn and perform, will give you the chance to observe and help all your students. Because scorekeepers for each contest will note some form of statistics, a cumulative record of some key performance indicators will be available, not only for feedback for students to improve, but also for assessment purposes. As the season progresses, you will not only see improvement in students but also have records that show their improvement.

Chapter Slides

Scorekeeping & Stats

AUTHENTIC ASSESSMENT

The structure of Sport Education seasons, which emphasize authentic competition, also allows for authentic assessments. Sport Education emphasizes authentic outcomes, which can be defined as the capability to do a task to its successful completion in a context that is relevant to how the task is done in the larger world (Siedentop, 1996). For educators who value authentic outcomes, the idea is to align instruction so students can demonstrate the outcome in the context in which it is appropriate (what we call contextualized performance capabilities). If a final exam exists, it is the performance itself.

> . . . we speak of such a final challenge as an "exhibition." It is a "test" in the sense that the big game on opening night is a "test." Unlike the conventional "final," the exhibition—like a piano recital or a play—lets the performer show off or "exhibit" what he or she knows. (Wiggins, 1987, p. 15)

In Sport Education, the "exhibitions" as referred to in Wiggins (1987) are balance beam routines, 3v3 volleyball championships, track and field culminating events, performing an aerobics dance routine before judges, and the like.

While end-of-season assessment is important because it marks the achievement of specific goals, Sport Education also offers the opportunity for regular assessment that can be used for feedback, marking progress, and contributing to a final assessment. We know that to judge a team's or an athlete's performance solely on a single performance does not provide a set of data that are as valid as performance across the length of a season.

Sport Education offers the continual opportunity to assess students in the appropriate contextual situation (e.g., the game, performance, or contest). Assessing students in tasks that are not gamelike makes less sense. While students are given a number of opportunities to practice techniques or tactics, the true test is the degree to which they are able to incorporate them into the game, contest, or performance situation. Because Sport Education seasons involve frequent participation in game, contest, and performance situations, and all those situations involve small teams or groups, your students will get many more opportunities to perform the techniques and tactics they are learning, allowing you more time to observe and assess student performance. When you use the small-sided games model, in which team performance is determined by the performances of all team members, you will create a situation in which students cannot hide and both the formal and informal contingencies will motivate them to learn and perform as well as possible. This situation is far different from the typical physical education setting in which large teams and low accountability for performance allow many students to participate only at a marginal level.

> *S*port Education provided an assessment focus for teachers to talk about assessment. All teachers became better able to identify issues and articulate positions on assessment. Sport Education provided an opportunity to reflect on alternative assessment techniques and appeared to change teacher attitudes to assessment.
>
> —Taggart, Brown, & Alexander, 1995 p. 15

In Sport Education, you can capture enough of your students' performance across a range of activities to be able to claim that an informative, accurate estimate of performance has been made. Because all of the roles students occupy are so important to the success of Sport Education, you must assess student performance in refereeing, scorekeeping, and performing a team administrative role as well as competing. Because students perform these roles during the season, the other advantage of Sport Education is that during one particular game, you can watch one group of students perform their refereeing and duty roles while observing another group of students perform in contests.

9 Assessing Student Roles

Teachers know when they are watching an activity performed well. They know what a well-played basketball game looks like—students create space, spread the floor, make appropriate passes, move to support teammates on defense, and dribble, pass, screen, rebound, and shoot with a modicum of skill. They know what a well-performed folk or aerobic dance routine looks like—students have mastered the steps and moves, and the performance meshes with the musical accompaniment. The entire dance flows to its conclusion. They know what a floor exercise routine looks like in gymnastics—they can see the elements chosen and how they fit together to make a total routine. These images should be your goals as a sport educator. They are authentic, and they tend to be valued by students and others who watch them learning to perform them. These kinds of goals are all within the reach of Sport Education teachers because the model allows for students to have sufficient time to learn and improve to the point at which they become familiar and comfortable performing the techniques and tactics in the applied setting.

PLANNING A WORKABLE ASSESSMENT SYSTEM

14 Chapter Slides

Building an assessment system for Sport Education requires three steps. The first is to identify outcomes that are authentic in the sense that they make clear to students the nature of the performance that is useful in the applied situation. The second is to develop assessment tools that provide valid information about those outcomes. The third is to use the data collected with the assessment tools to document the degree to which students have achieved the outcomes.

Step 1: Identify Outcomes

Planning for assessment begins with setting goals and asking the question, What do we want to see from the students at the end of the season? You must always answer this question specifically for the activity chosen for the season; that is, the outcomes will be different for a floor hockey season (a court invasion game) and for a badminton season (a court-divided game) and different still for a strength training season or a folk dance season. An advantage of the Sport Education format is that it allows for the pursuit of multiple goals, and also for each of those goals to be measured in authentic ways. The following list provides a template for identifying goals if you or your students are new to the Sport Education model.

- Goals related to knowledge about the key features of the game or activity (e.g., rules, history, traditions)
- Goals related to competent performance of officiating and scorekeeping roles that will be necessary depending on the activity chosen
- Goals related to beginning performance in other team roles (e.g., coach, manager)
- Goals related to the use of rudimentary techniques and tactics needed for the game or activity to be done well and enjoyed by all participants
- Goals related to student understanding and demonstration of behavior that is consistent with the fair play behavior system (see chapter 7)

In performance sports such as gymnastics, you may substitute the ability to design and perform routines for the use of tactics. If the season focuses on a fitness activity such as in-line skating, weight training, swimming, or aerobics, levels of improvement in fitness may be exchanged for the use of tactics.

If you and your students have experience in Sport Education, the template will become more sophisticated, as in the list that follows.

- More sophisticated game play performance, more complex tactics and techniques
- Evidence of leadership through more assertive and supportive performance in regular Sport Education roles and responsible participation on committees (e.g., sports board, judiciary committee, rules committee)
- A developed student capacity to examine issues related to fair play and equity opportunities and to show that they value these concepts in how they treat teammates and opponents

The global goal of Sport Education is to develop competent, literate, and enthusiastic sport players. The outcome templates we just identified are the means for contributing to those global goals. You can approach assessment for these outcomes using the following assessment categories: mastery of techniques, mastery of tactics, knowledge of the activity, knowledge and skills needed to perform nonplaying roles, and knowledge and value of fair play behavior.

Mastery of Techniques

A significant component of sport education is to develop competent performers. We know that one of the best predictors for students seeking out-of-school participation opportunities is confidence in their abilities to play well. Playing well, as described in chapter 2, means being in the right place at the right time (tactics) and then having the capacity to perform the right technique. The combination of tactics and techniques is what we call skilled play. Think of your own sport experiences. You are less likely to play in a recreational league in volleyball if you lack confidence in your ability to play, while you might be very attracted to a softball league if your techniques and tactics are solid.

As a sport education teacher, you will want students to be able to **execute the techniques** of the sport you are teaching. In volleyball they should be able to serve, pass, block, and spike. In a track and field season, they should put a shot with good form, take a smooth run-up and take-off in the long jump, and master the hop-step-jump sequence in the triple jump. In a weight training season, you would look for good form in various lifts. Notice that our emphasis is on the quality of the technical execution, as opposed to the outcome.

Mastery of Tactics

Competence is more than performing isolated techniques, and you should be assessing students on their ability to anticipate the flow of a contest and move into positions than enable them to perform the appropriate offensive or defensive technique. Anticipation and movement are what **tactics** are all about, from both offensive and defensive perspectives. For example, in soccer or basketball, a student will have to anticipate the offensive or defensive movement when they do not have control of the ball so as to get in a position of advantage for their team. If they get the ball, then they will have to decide correctly whether to dribble, pass, or shoot. Tactics can be divided into two categories. In the first category are tactics that are general in nature, for example, the concepts of moving to open spaces and floor or field balance in invasion games. In the second category are specific tactics related to specific offensive and defensive strategies, such as team movements in a zone defense in basketball.

Knowledge-Related Items

With regard to **knowledge,** students should be able to correctly identify the rules, history, and traditions of a game; they should be able to accurately score a contest; and they should know which penalties are appropriate when a foul is called. They should have a beginning knowledge of the tactics relevant to various games. This knowledge is highly generalizable within game categories. For example, the concept of off-the-ball movement and floor and field balance is relevant to all court and field invasion games. In addition, where relevant, students should be able to assess the skill and fitness requirements for successful competition. Students also profit from learning about the fitness specific to each kind of activity. You may assign a project, at an individual or a team level, that requires students to research the particular sport being studied and to identify ways in which they can improve their sport-specific fitness over a season. You may ask students to explore the contribution of various energy systems to successful performance in a sport, and to design a personal training program that matches those requirements.

Knowledge and Skills Needed to Perform Nonplaying Roles

Refereeing, coaching, managing, and other **nonplaying roles** each require certain skills. Referees need to learn how and when to move, how to make a call, and how to interact with players. Coaches need to know how to give instructions and feedback and how to appropriately motivate their team. Managers need to know how to plan and organize a small group to carry out assigned managerial tasks. While these are not high-level skills, students who are learning these roles deserve to have them explained and to be given opportunities to practice them with some feedback from you.

9

Assessing Personal &
Social Responsibility/
Assessing Fair Play

Developing and Valuing Fair Play Behavior

The approach to personal and social development described in chapter 7 focuses on fair play behavior. The goals of fair play in Sport Education are summarized as follows:

- Participate fully and responsibly.
- Give your best effort.
- Respect the rights and feelings of teammates and opponents.
- Be a good sport.
- Be helpful and not harmful.

It is important that you assess student performance related to these goals.

Full participation is a key element in Sport Education. Games are made friendly to students through developmentally appropriate modifications. While friendly games help in motivating students to take part fully, students need encouragement to do so. Team support is vital for achievement of this outcome. The evidence is compelling that typically nonparticipating students in physical education are much more likely to be involved in Sport Education because their teammates value their involvement (Carlson & Hastie, 1997).

A valued outcome of Sport Education is that students show a commitment to their team. This outcome can be demonstrated through students who always wear their team colors or uniform to class, who perform their roles reliably, and who contribute items to the team portfolio or team poster. Most important, the commitment to the team concept is shown by a willingness among team members to help and support one another in practice, in duty team roles, and in competitions.

> *I*f you're a bad player you can learn to be a good player, like before I couldn't run, I couldn't catch, and I couldn't throw and now I have sort of improved a little bit and it's really good of my team because everyone trusted me no matter what I did and they still throw it [the ball] to me no matter what.
>
> —Low-skilled ninth grade student, Australia

Because the social dimension of Sport Education is such a significant part of the overall model and a critical part to the success of a season, a legitimate outcome for students is to indeed accept and act on the advice given to them by their peers. Many students comment that this particular feature is a positive aspect of their participation. Students often see teachers as bossy and their peer coaches friendly. However, younger children or students experiencing Sport Education for the first time will need instruction and support from you to understand and act in ways that are helpful to teammates and to avoid behavior that is harmful to teammates. This aspect of behavior development is crucial to the success of the small learning group model that is at the heart of Sport Education.

Students must learn responsibility, and one way to do so is through successfully completing administrative roles. Students must also cooperate with directions, both from you and from their team coach and manager.

If you want students to take their nonplaying roles seriously, you need to hold them accountable for their performance in those roles. Just as it is possible for you to assess students completing their roles during team practices or in competition, it is also possible to build in an accountability or assessment system that involves significant **peer evaluations.** One such example is a peer referee report (see figure 9.1). Completed by the players on the participating teams, this checklist gives the teacher some feedback about the performance of the student referee. Because all students will be in the role of referee, they are likely to take the evaluation more seriously, knowing that they too will be evaluated.

Assessing Student Roles/By Students

Peer Assessment of Referee Performance

Team:_____   Final score:_____

Referee:_____

Answer questions as a team.
Be fair and honest.

1 = Poor
2 = Not bad
3 = Average
4 = Good
5 = Excellent

	1	2	3	4	5
The referee was fair and impartial.					
The referee knew the rules.					
The referee was clear in his/her explanations.					
Rate the overall job of this referee.					

Figure 9.1   Sample peer referee report.

Effort is a concept that younger students need to learn. They have to be shown what effort looks and feels like and provided frequent prompts about making the required effort. The appropriate meaning of effort during practice, in discharging duty team responsibilities, in discharging a team role such as manager or coach, and in competition, all have to be taught and emphasized, especially for young learners. Many teachers take the occasion of whole-class moments or closure activities to compliment students who have shown effort. Some use a signal system for students to indicate their perceived level of effort. A thumbs-up sign from a student will indicate that he or she thought they gave a great effort in class, while a thumbs-down sign would indicate they thought they might do better. A halfway thumb sign, which shakes up and down, indicates an undecided or partial response. Children soon become accurate monitors of their own effort levels, particularly when teachers reinforce the idea that everyone can have a bad day now and then, and that a goal is for everyone to work toward good effort.

When team portfolios are developed, students can be responsible for keeping a log of their participation and learning in their roles—some personal reflection about their success and learning, and even peer evaluations concerning their contribution to the team. They can also produce logs of their effort level for each class as a self-evaluation.

Team Portfolios

Assessing Personal & Social Responsibility

Respecting the rights and feelings of teammates and classmates means that students need to display tolerance of and support for their peers on individual, team, and class levels. This area of Sport Education is one in which the extended time provides the extended instructional opportunities to teach toward peer tolerance, acceptance, and cooperation. Studies have demonstrated significant improvements in students' levels of positive interpersonal interactions and leadership statements when an assessment system has existed for them. One teacher had all students complete a self-evaluation of their social behaviors after each game. The questions are shown in table 9.1.

Table 9.1   Sample Student Self-Evaluation of Social Behavior

Circle the statement that best describes how you played during this game.

1. I argued with the referee's calls.	Never	Sometimes	Mostly	Always
2. I fussed at my teammates if they made a mistake.	Never	Sometimes	Mostly	Always
3. I praised my teammates if they tried hard.	Never	Sometimes	Mostly	Always
4. I was a good winner, and I supported and praised the other team when we did not win.	Never	Sometimes	Mostly	Always
5. I showed enthusiasm and gave my best effort during the game.	Never	Sometimes	Mostly	Always

Students need to learn the rules and then play by them. Part of being a good sport is respecting the referees and officials. You should note infractions of rules, and both positive and negative instances of student behavior related to referees' and officials' decisions during contests. Self-evaluations, such as the one shown in table 9.1, are valuable here. Students should be shown ways that are appropriate to express appreciation for their teammates and their opponents. They must go beyond the ritualistic ways of shaking hands after contests, even though those rituals are also important. Many Sport Education teachers have created daily and seasonal **fair play awards** for individuals and for teams.

Awards/Fair Play Awards

You should help your students learn what it means to be helpful and not harmful. Teasing and bullying are often too evident in sport and physical activity settings; indeed, trash talk has evidently reached a level of acceptance in some professional sports. Thus, you should develop and implement a system for resolving conflicts. These methods should be age appropriate (see chapter 7 for examples). Assess students on their utilization of the conflict resolutions adopted for the Sport Education program you have developed.

Step 2: Develop Assessment Tools

Once you have set goals, you must design tools to assess achievement of those goals. A number of tools are clearly suitable for assessing students in Sport Education. You can develop written tests and assignments to test knowledge. You can develop checklists, rating scales, peer assessment experiences, journals, and event tasks for any of the behavioral objectives you wish to see during game play or during the conduct of administrative and duty tasks.

In planning the assessment tools, remember that assessment in Sport Education is integrated across the entire season. You must determine the lesson component and season phase during which the instrument will be used, how much time it will take to complete, and the number of times it will be used during a season.

If you have students who are experienced in Sport Education, you may involve them in developing the tools for specific situations. For example, you may ask students to develop a checklist that measures fair play or the contribution to one's team. In addition, nothing suggests that self-assessment is not a legitimate objective for measuring sport education outcomes. Tables 9.2 through 9.5 provide an extensive list of outcome measures in Sport Education and the appropriate tools available to assess them. Following each table are one or two completed sample tools.

Table 9.2   Assessment Tools for Measuring Techniques and Tactics

Type of information measured	Checklist	Rating scale	Participation log	Journal	Game statistics	Game analysis systems
Correct weightlifting techniques	X	X	X		X	
Correct spotting techniques (weightlifting or gymnastics)	X	X				
Correct sequence of steps in a dance	X	X			X	
Skill production (e.g., golf putting or gymnastics skills)	X	X	X	X	X	
Use of tactics during game play	X	X		X	X	X

For teachers who wish to be sophisticated in their measurement of game play, Gréhaigne, Godbout, and Bouthier (1999) have developed what is known as an efficiency index. This score provides an overall indication of a player's performance during a game. The formula for this index is easy to understand. Simply, one adds all those positive things a player does in a game, and divides this score by the total of the counterproductive actions. For example, in a Frisbee game, the positive actions would include interceptions or knocked downs, catches from one's own team, successful passes to a teammate, and scoring passes. The counterproductive actions would include incomplete throws (those that that hit the ground or flew out of bounds), as well as intercepted and knocked down passes, and passes from a teammate that were dropped. In volleyball, positive actions would include spike winners, service aces, dig saves, and blocks, while errors might include uncontrolled passes, hits that fail to cross the net or travel out of bounds, and missed serves.

To provide a more manageable score, Gréhaigne, Godbout, and Bouthier suggested adding 10 points to the denominator of the fraction. The efficiency index, then, is calculated as follows:

$$\text{Efficiency index} = \text{positive actions}/(10 + \text{negative actions})$$

All you have to do as a teacher is to identify those features of the game that you wish to include as positive and negative actions.

Pickleball Game Play Rating Scale

Select the term that best matches the student's ability at each of the components of pickleball. Total the scores for each component to give a final score.

	5	4	3	2
Serving	**Potent:** Used as an attacking weapon—with variance in placement, speed, and spin	**Reliable:** Consistent and firm, but without significant placement.	**Passive:** Aim is to simply get the ball in play.	**Inconsistent:** Serve only sometimes is put in play.
Ground strokes	**Flat and driven:** Hits flat over the net, uses change of pace, and can lob	**Mainly firm:** Hits flat over the net, but with low threat	**Loopy and arched:** Ball is lobbed back to the opponent with little deliberate change of pace	**Inconsistent:** Ground strokes only sometimes put in play
Ball placement	**To spaces:** Ball is hit to the corners and either short or long depending on opponent's court position	**Some active placement:** Is able to place the ball to spaces when it is hit directly to the player	**Returns consistently:** Returns ball in most cases, but with little account for placement	**Survival focus:** Aim of ball placement is to simply get the ball back over the net, without concern for a specific spot on the court
Volleying	**Active weapon:** Uses volleys as an offensive tool; moves to the net to volley when opponent is under pressure	**Controlled:** Can use a volley if it is the appropriate shot, but not as if it has been planned for and set up	**Reactive:** Volleys ball when it is hit directly toward the player; a reactive shot rather than a planned one	**Does not use:** Does not use volleying during games
Off-the-ball movement	**Anticipates:** Plans movements a play ahead to be where the opponent will return to the ball	**Returns to center:** Moves to the center of the court after most shots, attempting not to be stranded	**Reacts to the ball:** Court position determined by the shot making of the opponent, rather than a planned one	**Static:** Player does not respond to placement of the ball; remains in one place on the court and strikes the ball from there when possible

Example of an assessment tool to measure techniques and tactics. Similar forms can also be found on the CD-ROM in Resource 9, Assessing Techniques and Tactics.

Gymnastics Compulsory Routine Partner Checksheet

Determine whether your partner is performing the "blue" or "green" routine. Using the check system given below, rate your partner's performance on each of the 12 parts of the routine.

Check System:

- –   Requires a heavy spot, falls, or performs with large/medium error

- +   Can perform skill, but has small form error

- ✔   Perfect performance

Blue routine

- ❏   1. Acknowledge the judge
- ❏   2. Straight body stretch
- ❏   3. Step forward into a lunge (hold 3 counts)
- ❏   4. Forward roll to stand:
    - A. On incline mat
    - B. On a flat mat
- ❏   5. Tripod balance (hold 3 counts, then feet down to stretch stand)
- ❏   6. Chassé
- ❏   7. Pivot one half turn on balls of feet
- ❏   8. Back roll to straddle out:
    - A. On incline mat
    - B. On flat mat
- ❏   9. Straight jump
- ❏   10. Knee lunge (hold 3 counts)
- ❏   11. Stand—stretch to end
- ❏   12. Acknowledge the judge

Green routine

- ❏   1. Acknowledge the judge
- ❏   2. Straight body stretch
- ❏   3. Step forward into a lunge (hold 3 counts)
- ❏   4. Cartwheel to lunge
- ❏   5. Headstand (hold 3 counts, then feet down to stretch stand)
- ❏   6. Chassé
- ❏   7. Pivot one half turn on balls of feet
- ❏   8. Back roll to stand
- ❏   9. Jump one half turn
- ❏   10. Knee lunge (hold 3 counts)
- ❏   11. Stand—stretch to end
- ❏   12. Acknowledge the judge

Example of an assessment tool to measure techniques and tactics. Similar forms can also be found on the CD-ROM in Resource 9, Assessing Techniques and Tactics.

Table 9.3 Assessment Tools to Measure Fair Play Behaviors

Type of information measured	Written test	Assignment	Worksheet	Checklist	Rating scale	Journal	Presentation	Work task
Rules of the sport	X	X	X				X	
History of the sport	X	X	X				X	
Traditions of the sport	X	X	X				X	
How to keep score	X						X	X
Definitions of statistics	X							
Development of a personal training plan for fitness development		X		X	X	X	X	
Identifying control points on an orienteering map	X		X					X

Badminton Scoring Test

Fill in the blanks for each of the following questions.

1. In doubles and men's singles a game is won by the first side to score _____ points.

2. In women's singles a game is won by the first side to score _____ points.

3. Explain the concept of setting.

_____

_____

_____

4. If the game has been set, the side first scoring _____ additional points wins the game.

5. If the game has not been set, the side scoring _____ wins the game.

Example of an assessment tool to measure knowledge of an activity.

Orienteering Work Task

Examine the orienteering map, taking particular note of the symbols at each of the control points. Color in each of these control points, using the correct color as determined from the following table.

Color	Feature
Black	Rock features and linear features such as roads, trails, and fences as well as other man-made features (for example, ruins and buildings)
Brown	Landforms such as contour lines, small knolls, ditches, earthbanks
Blue	Water features: lakes, ponds, rivers, streams, marshes
Yellow	Vegetation—specifically, open or unforested land
Green	Vegetation that slows down the passage of an orienteer
White	Forest with little or no undergrowth—forest that an orienteer can run through

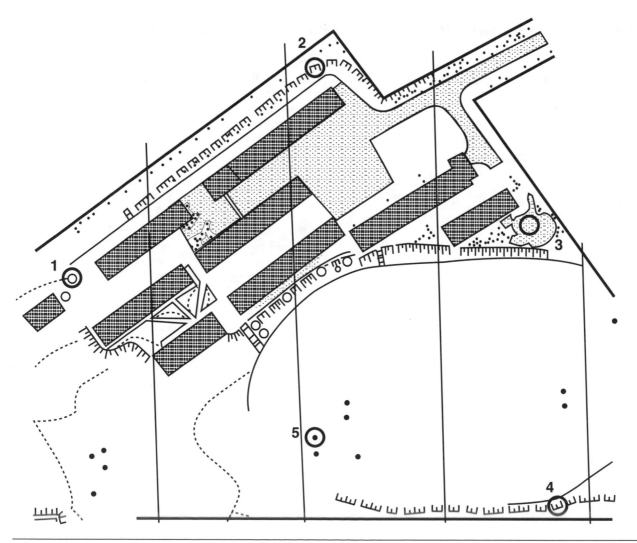

Example of an assessment tool to measure knowledge of an activity.

Table 9.4 Assessment Tools for Measuring Performance in Nonplaying Roles

Type of information measured	Checklist	Rating scale	Journal	Presentation	Work task
Officiating during competition	X	X			
Completing scoresheets	X	X			X
Completing statistics sheets	X	X			X
Completing judging sheets	X	X			X

Table 9.5 Assessment Tools for Measuring Fair Play Behaviors

Type of information measured	Checklist	Rating scale	Worksheet	Journal	Participation log
Enthusiastic participation	X	X		X	X
Seeks opportunities to learn and practices hard to improve skills or fitness				X	X
Seek new opportunities to participate outside physical education time			X	X	X
Accepts and acts upon advice	X	X			
Assumes responsibility for one's designated role	X	X		X	
Cooperates in ways that enhance class management	X	X			
Displays tolerance toward peers on an individual, team, and class level	X	X		X	
Exhibits a commitment to the team	X	X		X	
Use of conflict resolution strategies	X	X		X	

Officiating Rating Scale

Name: _____   Team: _____

Referee	Always 1 point	Mostly 0.5 point	Sometimes 0 points
Shows all signals at appropriate times			
Shows correct signals			
Makes signals clear and visible to all players			
Makes precise and exact hand motions			
Uses whistle			
Total			

Scorer	Always 1 point	Mostly 0.5 point	Sometimes 0 points
Keeps accurate and complete statistics			
Announces every change of score			
Makes clear and loud score announcements			
Announces point			
Assists referee in making calls			
Total			

Team Statistician	Always 1 point	Mostly 0.5 point	Sometimes 0 points
Collects game results promptly			
Enters results in team binder following each game			
Keeps records in order			
Communicates team stats to team frequently			
Provides team publicist with updates (if applicable)			
Total			

Example of an assessment tool to measure performance in non-playing roles. Similar forms can be found on the CD-ROM, Resource 9, Assessing Student Roles/By Teacher.

Out-of-Class Activity Participation Log: Ultimate Frisbee Season

Select at least four days this week in which you will participate in some physical activity outside of class that will improve your ability to play Ultimate Frisbee. The activity could relate to improvements in aerobic fitness or improvements in skill. Be realistic in setting your goals and planning these activities. Choose activities that you enjoy and can do with a friend or family member.

The aim is to accumulate between 30 to 60 minutes of physical activity each day.

Weekly activity plan and record

Day/date	Activity	Objective (skill/fitness)	Time (min.)	Alone/others
Example 04/06/04	Jogged to the park and home. Threw Frisbee with friends.	Aerobic fitness Skill	15 minutes 30 minutes	Alone Jessica/Allen
Monday				
Tuesday				
Wednesday				
Thursday				
Friday				
Saturday				
Sunday				

Student signature: _____ Date:_____

Parent/guardian signature:_____ Date:_____

Teacher signature:_____ Date:_____

Example of an assessment tool to measure out-of-class activity participation.

Role Responsibility Checklist: Dance Season

Directions

Determine your role and corresponding responsibilities for the day's lesson. At the end of the lesson you will be asked to determine the responsibilities that you successfully completed. For each responsibility successfully completed, place a check [✔] in the box. For each responsibility that you did not successfully complete place a zero [0] in the box.

Roles and responsibilities	LESSON											
	1	2	3	4	5	6	7	8	9	10	11	12
Choreographer												
• Leads dance troupe practice	✔											
• Assists teacher when needed	0											
• Assists teammates in learning dance moves	✔											
Fitness Trainer												
• Selects appropriate warm-up activities												
• Leads troupe warm-up												
• Reports injuries to teacher												
• Aids teacher in administering first-aid												
Dance Season Committee Member												
• Assists in selecting dance troupes												
• Summarizes the application dance scores												
• Monitors allotted dance times during contests												
• Judges Dance Fever application tasks												
Disc Jockey (DJ)												
• Maintains and monitors audio equipment												
• Chooses appropriate music for troupe routines												
• Records team strategy practice												
Master of Ceremonies												
• Introduces troupe members, dance themes, and musical selections												
• Attends to management of practice and application tasks												
Reviewer/Critic												
• Publicizes records via newsletters, etc.												
• Reports progress daily to troupe members												
• Assumes role responsibilities for absent troupe members												

Example of an assessment tool to measure student role performance. Similar form can be found on the CD-ROM, Resource 9, Assessing Student Roles/By Students.

Reprinted from Assessing Student Outcomes in Sport Education, with permission from the National Association for Sport and Physical Education (NASPE), 1900 Association Drive, Reston, VA 20191, USA.

Step 3: Document Student Outcomes

Once you have developed assessment tools and collected data, you need to design a report form where students' achievements can be recorded. Some teachers have turned to students developing **team portfolios** to document their participation in sport education. Kinchin (2001) provides one example of such a portfolio that was designed to show students' achievement in relation to the objectives of competence, literacy, and enthusiasm (see table 9.6).

Table 9.6   Assessing Achievement of Sport Education Goals

Artifact	Competent	Literate	Enthusiastic
Self-assessment of performance	X		
Rules test		X	
Fair play awards			X
Peer skills test	X		
Role evaluation		X	
Activity log/diary			X

At the high school level, physical education exists in an academic setting in which grades are required and certain expectations for course materials exist. In some cases, grading can be based on a task-completion format. That is, students are required to complete a number of tasks at a certain standard. Dugas (1994) reports that "a task-completion format results in a form of student-directed quality control." That is, "if students have tasks as officials, scorekeepers, and referees, for example, it is the student feedback that results in quality performance. If student scorekeepers do not accomplish their task well, they will be quick to find out as student peers ask about their scores" (p. 108). In the Dugas system, even the written exam is carried out as a task-completion task. That is, students need to achieve an 80-percent accuracy rate on the test for it to count. One example of a grading system based on task completion is shown in figure 9.2.

Sample Course Evaluation

Written exam (50 points)	50
League play (8 at 15 points each)	120
Officiating (4 at 10 points each)	40

Figure 9.2   Sample course evaluation grading breakdown based on a task-completion format.

You can assess a student coach on a number of dimensions, which all relate to what the student coach can do. These things include planning, teaching skills, organization, and provision of positive team support. Desirable teaching skills for a student coach are that he or she be able to demonstrate skills, ask questions, provide feedback, and have students actively participate in drills. Of course, these outcomes are valued for any teacher, but we know that student coaches tend to spend more time playing games with their teams than teaching skills. While teachers spend more time in refining and extending tasks, peer coaches spend more time in organization, demonstration, and application tasks (Hastie, 2000).

LEAGUE SCORING SYSTEMS

To date, this chapter has examined how we assess individual students relating to your desired outcomes for a season. In designing a season plan, you also need to examine how you are going to determine a champion team.

One of the significant differences in Sport Education in comparison with school and community sport is the way in which you determine the overall season champion. In professional leagues and high school sport, the only thing that counts is the win–loss record. In Sport Education, the teacher is given significant liberty in incorporating a number of different objectives into the determination of the champion team. Figure 9.3 shows an example from an elementary setting where teams competed for the All Sport Award.

The league table from an eighth grade Frisbee season also shows how a team's win–loss record is not the sole indicator of team success (table 9.7). Table 9.7 shows how a team that wins but does not exhibit the appropriate personal and

All Sport Award Point System

Daily teamwork points: (30 possible points, 1 earned in each category on a daily basis)

- 10—Warm-ups/cool-downs properly completed by all team members
- 10—All team members dressed appropriately and no tardies
- 10—Team participation in class activities

Team cognitive points: (30 possible, awarded on an all-or-none basis in each category)

- 10—Refereeing
- 10—Notebooks completed and turned in on time
- 10—Tests and worksheets turned in on time and all team members get a passing grade (70 percent or better)

Fair play points: (40 initial points)

- 1 point deducted for warning by teacher or referee
- 2 points deducted for time-out by teacher or yellow card
- 3 points deducted for repeated time-out, red card, or technical foul

Tournament points

- 1 point for playing cooperatively
- 1 point for each win
- 1/2 point for each tie

Figure 9.3 The All Sport Award is a yearlong award given to the team that accumulates the highest percentage of points in four areas: daily teamwork, cognitive tasks, fair play, and tournament points.

social behaviors, such as playing fair, can be matched in total points by a team that lost its game but showed all the desirable positive attributes of fair play and persistence. Notice how the Devils won the fewest games, but finished third overall, their score boosted by excellent team organization and duty team performance. Likewise, the winningest team in the class (Rangers) finished well down the table in fifth place, mainly because of low fair play points.

Table 9.7   Sample League Standings

Team	Win points (5/win)	Tie points (3/tie)	Fair play (3/match)	Organization (2/match)	Duty team (5/match)	Total
Eagles	25	6	30	20	25	106
Tigers	25	0	30	20	22	97
Devils	15	6	28	20	25	94
Scorpions	20	3	26	17	25	91
Rangers	30	0	20	16	23	89
Lions	15	3	28	18	24	88

The example just shown is but one of many designs that you might use. All you need to do is to go through a three-step process:

1. Decide which features you want to see or which are particularly important to your season.
2. Provide a weighting for those outcomes.
3. Design the instruments by which you will collect that information.

The easiest variable to manipulate is the match play points. In head-to-head competition such as basketball or soccer, you may allocate 2 points for a win, 1 for a tie, and 0 for a loss. In Australian football, the ratio is win = 4, 2 = tie, 0 = loss, while in soccer, the common convention is win = 3, draw = 1, loss = 0. The National Hockey League now uses a system whereby teams who finish the game in regulation as a tie scoring 1 point each, but if a team wins in overtime it collects another point.

In dual sports, where teams might play a number of singles and doubles matches against another team, the points may simply be the number of matches won by each team. For example, in a five-player league involving three singles and one doubles match, a team could score anywhere from 0 to 4 points, depending on its total wins. If teams are tied at 2–2, you might give a bonus point to the team that won more total points; information which is available from the scoresheets and should be reported by the statistician.

A Note on Fair Play

Fair play must be prominent in any seasonal scoring system. In many elementary settings, teams begin with a designated number of fair play points and receive deductions if they break fair play rules. For example, a teacher warning might cost 1 point, and a time-out may cost 2. In many international sports, referees use yellow cards to warn participants of questionable play or rule infractions and

**Assessing Personal &
Social Responsibility/
Assessing Fair Play**

use red cards to signal a penalty. This card model can be easily adapted to Sport Education activities.

Some **fair play** systems work on a referee checklist, where the number of yes statements equals the total points given. In other cases, the referee may award 2-1-0 points. For a team to score 2 points, not only does it need to play fair (i.e., not argue with officials), but it must also provide positive comments to its teammates and recognize good play by the opponents. A team playing within the rules and acting in a neutral manner may score 1 point, while a team that displays negative reactions would score 0.

> *I*n a fourth grade ultimate Frisbee unit, a student teacher added a good sportsmanship monitor as another student role for the duty team. The monitor listed and recorded examples of fair play during game[s]. At end of lesson, monitors read names and deeds of those students who exemplified fair play. The names were then posted on [a] display board.
>
> —Professor, USA

In some leagues, teachers will require teams to exhibit a certain level of fair play to become eligible for the final play-offs. For example, where teams are awarded 3 possible points each day, a useful cut-off is 70 percent. That is, a team needs to average better than 2 out of 3 (66 percent) positive outcomes for fair play throughout the course of a season to qualify. In leagues that have adopted this strategy, it is not uncommon to see captains reminding their teams (and specific players in particular) that they need to be aware of the team's current fair play status, and to be very disciplined in their interactions with the officials.

Power Ratings

In some elementary settings, teachers enjoy using the concept of power ratings. Very similar to the format used in figure 9.4, power ratings are points given by the teacher to teams for accomplishing tasks in the managerial system. Power rating points can be awarded in the following cases. One point is awarded if

- within 3 minutes of arriving at class, a team is in its designated home space performing its warm-up led by the fitness leader;
- its manager returns a team's equipment to the appropriate place in the gym at the end of a lesson;
- the team moves in an orderly fashion from its home space to the playing area promptly and is ready to begin games on time; or
- the team displays the appropriate post-match protocols (e.g., lining up and shaking hands with the opposition).

The power ratings are added to the scores obtained from match play. In one elementary school season of flag football, teams earned one point for each touchdown they scored during play, with up to 4 possible power rating points added depending on achievement of class protocols. The **team power rating** system allows all teams to score the maximum possible for a single lesson, and also serves to keep the league totals close.

**Assessing Student
Roles**

When using any scoring system it is critical that these data are clearly made public for all students to see. Having an up-to-date scoreboard is critical if students are to become enthusiastic about the importance of the nonplaying tasks. Having

Team Power Rating

Teams	Tasks	Season days 1	2	3	4	5	6	7	8	9	10	
		Date										
Sharks	Quick team start	1	1	1	1		1	1	1		1	
	Equipment returned	1	1	1	1		1	1	1		1	
	Efficient transition to game	−1	0	1	0		1	1	1		0	
	Post-game behavior	1	1	1	0		1	0	1		2	Total
	Daily total	**2**	**3**	**4**	**2**	**0**	**4**	**3**	**4**	**0**	**4**	**26**
Tigers	Quick team start	1	1	1		1	1	1		1	1	
	Equipment returned	1	1	1		1	1	1		1	1	
	Efficient transition to game	1	1	0		1	1	1		1	1	
	Post-game behavior	1	0	1		1	1	1		1	0	Total
	Daily total	**4**	**3**	**3**	**0**	**4**	**4**	**4**	**0**	**4**	**3**	**29**
Islanders	Quick team start	1	1		1	1	1		1	1	1	
	Equipment returned	1	1		1	1	1		1	1	1	
	Efficient transition to game	1	1		0	1	1		1	1	1	
	Post-game behavior	1	1		1	1	1		1	1	0	Total
	Daily total	**4**	**4**	**0**	**3**	**4**	**4**	**0**	**4**	**4**	**3**	**30**

Figure 9.4 Sample team power ratings format.

these points as part of determining the season champions, but not having the system public, significantly reduces the authenticity of the season.

The systems described up to this point are used to determine the overall season champion. This does not preclude your having awards for various competition winners, such as the team scoring the most touchdowns or the winners of the early-season 2v2 competition. You may also use the data collected to give awards to the **best duty team,** the team with the **greatest levels of fair play,** or the **best officials.**

10

Awards/Non-Player Role Awards

Assessment is a crucial component of good instruction. The best assessment is ongoing in the sense that it is embedded in the daily activities of the class, rather than special in the sense that a mid-term test is on a day set aside solely for assessment. Point systems work well. Teams will work to earn points toward a championship. As students mature and get more experience in Sport Education, they can help create the point system, thus establishing even more ownership for their involvement.

We have provided extensive information on the kinds of assessment that might be done in Sport Education and methods for conducting these assessments. We do not to suggest that you have to assess everything formally with an instrument.

Informal self-assessments that occur at a critical moment (e.g., thumbs-up, and thumbs-down signs to indicate level of support or effort) show students that you are observing them and that you expect a fair self-assessment. Informal comments in a class closure segment that have an assessment purpose are also valuable because they indicate clearly to students that you are observing them and that you will provide feedback to them on these important behaviors. As students become more experienced with the Sport Education model, evidence suggests that they will become quite good at assessing their own efforts and will accept such assessment as a valuable aspect of their learning experience.

Chapter 10

Making Sport Education Festive

Festivity is one of the primary characteristics of Sport Education (see chapter 1). It is included as a primary characteristic in defining Sport Education and differentiating it from how sport is more typically taught in physical education programs for two reasons. First, sport is most often festive in the many different ways and places it is undertaken internationally, but it is seldom festive the way it is taught and practiced in physical education. It is not just the obvious sport festivals that have this characteristic in abundance; that is, not just the Olympic Games, World Cup soccer, or the NFL Super Bowl. Every summer evening we pass baseball diamonds where Little League teams are competing. They are dressed in uniforms. Parents and other siblings form an audience that is enthusiastic about the play on the field. The quality of play differs dramatically depending on the age group involved, but in all cases a note of festivity surrounds the competition. We also see a 65 and older softball league in the local area and that has similar signs of festivity.

14
Chapter Slides

In the United States, Friday night high school football has become a sport institution with clear festival characteristics. Players run on to the field under a large school banner. Cheerleaders spark the crowd's enthusiasm. The starting line-ups are introduced as players run onto the field to the cheers of their supporters. The national anthem is often played prior to the game. The school band plays for cheers throughout the game and does a special performance at half-time. In many towns, it is likely that a broadcast of the game could be heard on local radio. The results of the game are available in the local newspaper the next day, with particular notice paid to players who performed well and gave great effort.

A local 10K road race attracts 1,300 runners on a Saturday morning. A crowd gathers to cheer them off at the start line and local residents line the streets through which the race is run, cheering on all the competitors, not just the front-runners, but also the age-group runners and those in the wheelchair division. Every runner who finishes the race gets a ribbon. The place winners in age groups (typically by five-year increments from 20 to 65) get trophies. All of these sporting events have a measure of festivity that adds to their importance and makes them more enjoyable for participants and spectators alike.

A second reason festivity became a primary defining characteristic of Sport Education is that it helps to make the experience significant to the participants, thus increasing the likelihood that they may pursue sport and physical activity outside of the school physical education program. In many places in the world, a primary goal of physical education has become to influence the lifestyle choices that youngsters make—to increase the likelihood that they will adopt physically active lifestyles. To maintain a healthful, physically active lifestyle requires that youngsters value an activity and want to seek it out so they can continue participation. To come to value an activity, students must have had some significant experiences that motivate them to continue to pursue the activity further. Making the sport experience more festive is an important way to increase its significance to those taking part. The experience of a Sport Education teacher described in the next quotation is a good example of what valuing can mean in action.

When children participate in Sport Education for several seasons, they become adept at organizing and implementing their own sport involvement. I recall how amazed I was several years ago when I organized an intramural floor hockey tournament as an enrichment activity (we hadn't done floor hockey in physical education). Students organized themselves into teams and volunteered for referee duties. From the first day of the tournament, teams were in the gym ahead of schedule and ready to go at the scheduled time. Captains who had been elected took charge and made sure that positions were covered. Transitions with substitutes went smoothly and without argument. All students played an equal amount of time. Teams frequently came to me to ask for extra practice time with the equipment. It was one of those experiences where you realize that what you try to achieve sometimes does get done.

—Darnell, 1994, p. 71

In the United States interscholastic sport has provided significant experiences for many girls and boys. Club sports have done similarly in other parts of the world. However, students in physical education seldom view their experience as exciting or valuable. Quite to the contrary, in many places physical education is not only viewed as insignificant by students but far too often as an experience to be avoided, especially for adolescents in those crucial years when they are forming the value structures that will carry them into young adulthood. This idea is particularly true for less-skilled students and girls, who are often marginalized and unsuccessful in physical education. One recent study in Canada reported that girls disliked physical education so much that they tried to find ways to avoid it (Olafson, 2002). Sport Education has been proven again and again to be one good way to make a sport-based curriculum more significant to less-skilled students and for girls. Festivity is one of the characteristics of the Sport Education model that increases its potential for motivating students.

14
Chapter Slides

DEVELOPING A FESTIVE DAILY ENVIRONMENT FOR SPORT EDUCATION

Your goal should be to make the Sport Education experience festive on a daily basis. Do not assume that festivity is important only in a championship game at the end of a season; it is not just the culminating event that has a festive atmosphere. Strive to make the daily environment for learning and competing as festive as possible. All of the ways that we describe how teachers have made their Sport Education classes more festive have actually been done by teachers we know or by teachers who have communicated to us their enthusiasm for the Sport Education model and what it has meant to them and their students. We are not suggesting that you utilize all of these ideas, but rather we present enough of them so you can choose among them for ideas that best fit your situation. We will not be surprised if you think of some new ways to make things special for your students.

Teams

Putting students on teams that persist for at least the full length of the season creates affiliation, which is another primary characteristic of Sport Education. You can make teams more special for students in many ways, thus adding to their sense of belonging and their feelings of responsibility to do their part for their team. (See the Affiliation section in chapter 4.) Teams should have names, and students, within reason, should be able to choose the names for their teams. Each team can have a spot on the **bulletin board** to post their team results and performance statistics. Teams can also choose colors. We have numerous examples at the elementary level in which parents of children have made team shirts. Teachers can also take team pictures and post them at the team space on the bulletin board. Again, students should be able to create the team pose they would like for their team picture. Team publicists can develop and post individual player profiles.

Banners/Bulletin Board Banner Samples

> *T*he girls expressed to me a couple of times that they were planning as part of a team, so it was important for them to improve their skills to be part of their team.
>
> —High school teacher, Australia

   Teams typically have assigned spaces in the gymnasium or on the playing field. They go to their team space at the start of class and fulfill whatever entry routine (see page 89) their teacher uses, be it a warm-up or a skill drill. Teams can also be encouraged to practice in nonattached school time. Oftentimes, middle and high school teachers will have open gym times during extended lunch periods. Many teachers include such extra practice as a way to earn points toward a seasonal championship. In some variations of Sport Education, teachers have had teams represent countries, as in **Olympic Sport** or World Cup soccer. In these variations, teams adopt the flag, colors, and **anthems** of the nations they represent. All of these efforts reinforce team identity and make the experience more significant for the students.

Olympics

National Anthems

Awards

Awards abound in Sport Education. It is important that you find ways to recognize hard work, good performance, improvement, victories, and fair play. Many teachers end each class session with a class meeting in which various examples of good performance and fair play are pointed out. Good performance, of course, does not just mean players who performed well or teams that showed good tactical awareness, but also referees who kept games going well and called penalties appropriately. Teachers also can recognize duty teams that got players and equipment to the right places in a timely manner and then scored and refereed games

Fair Play Resources

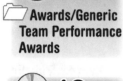

Awards/Generic Team Performance Awards

Awards/Fair Play Awards

Chapter Slides

well. Of particular importance is recognizing examples of fair play (see chapter 7). Students learn the most about the meaning of fair play by having examples pointed out to them and having those who show exemplary fair play recognized for it. Students and teams that get recognized during and at the end of class do not necessarily get trophies or certificates; rather, they get recognized in front of their classmates and publicly praised for their effort and performance. It is, of course, quite possible to have a fair play bulletin board on which you post the names of students who have been singled out for exemplary **fair play behavior.**

End-of-season awards are also an important part of Sport Education. Awards may be **certificates** and trophies of some kind. Some teachers have organized a committee of representatives from each team to plan and create awards for their sport season. This approach works particularly well to serve a cross-disciplinary curriculum model, in which students might do projects in an art class that serve the Sport Education season. Coaches who fulfill their responsibilities should be recognized with a coaching award, often as a result of fulfilling a coaching contract that they sign at the start of the season. Seasonal **fair play awards** are powerful in reinforcing the importance of those concepts and actions. An award for the most improved team gives recognition to another important concept, that of persevering in trying to improve as a group. And, of course, team performance will be recognized. **Team performance** will mean something different in the different point systems you have developed to determine the seasonal champion. Victories will obviously be a big part of determining the champion, but we have many examples of seasons in which the team with the most victories was not the champion. This may be because they lost fair play points or did not fulfill other obligations as duty team or did not get as many points as they could have for things such as practicing outside of class. You can recognize the champion team and the runner-up. These team awards go to the entire team even though each team might have had an A, B, and C team in the seasonal competition that was graded for different skill levels. If the competition format is graded, it is possible to not only recognize the overall champion and runner-up, but also the within-grade champions and runners-up. See figure 10.1 for ideas of awards and presentations.

DEVELOPING CULMINATING EVENTS

Sport Education seasons close with a culminating event that should be the most festive of all the days of the season. The nature of the culminating event will depend on the sport and how the competition is organized. We want to emphasize that you have many ways to create a culminating event that involves all of the students, not just the two top teams. For example, if you have used a graded competition format, with three class teams that each have A, B, and C teams competing, you can have a grand final competition in each of the divisions; that is, an A final, a B final, and a C final.

*F*or my handball season's culminating event, each team will have a song of their choice (with my approval), and they will play the song as they enter the gym and have 20 seconds of the song to do a dance or some kind of grand entrance. It should be very entertaining and will be video recorded for the students to review.

—Middle school student teacher, USA

Ideas for Awards and Presentations

Find ways to recognize and reward activities and roles you want students to do well. The following can be recognized and rewarded daily, weekly, and for the season.

- Outstanding fair play incidents
- Hard working teams during technique practice
- Efficient duty teams
- Improved uses of tactics during game play
- Quality refereeing
- Creative team cheers
- Accurate scorekeeping
- Most improved team
- Champions and runners-up for each competition

Create awards specific to the sport or activity for that season.

- "Top blocker" award for volleyball
- "Defender" awards for best execution of defensive tactics
- "Top assister" awards for most assists
- "Best builder" awards for acrosport competitions
- "I did it" awards for students who meet goals in fitness season
- "Top lifter" awards by weight class in strength training season
- "Top team scorer" awards
- "Most improved" for times and distances in track and field season

Figure 10.1 Awards can be sport-specific or they can be used to acknowledge effort and performance.
Adapted from Sport Education in Physical Education (SEPEP) materials, Perth, Western Australia.

As noted in chapter 6, another example of a culminating event is to have the class do a series of technique or **skill challenges.** Each team has representatives who complete the various challenges. Figure 10.2 shows an example of a teacher-organized Frisbee Olympics at the conclusion of a disc golf season.

10
Culminating Events/
One-Day Skill
Challenges

If the event is held within the confines of the regular class schedule, the culminating event may take several class sessions to complete. Championship games in various divisions (e.g., singles, doubles, and mixed doubles in tennis or badminton) might take several class sessions followed by an awards and recognition session on the final day of the season. Sport Education has become sufficiently important in many programs that special time is scheduled for a culminating event. The Super Bowl Day at Ogletree shown in figure 10.3 is an example from a middle school coed touch football season.

Following are some additional ideas for end-of-season culminating events. They come from various places around the world and show the imagination teachers have in creating end-of-season events that become significant experiences for the students. (We acknowledge two sources for some of these ideas. First is Grant, Sharp, & Siedentop [1992]. The second is the teacher materials prepared for the Sport Education in Physical Education Project (SEPEP) by the Sport and Physical Activity Research Centre at Edith Cowan University in Perth, Western Australia.)

Frisbee Olympics

- One team member will be a recorder for each event.
- Remaining team members must compete in at least one event each.
- Every team will enter four team members per event.

Events and Descriptions

Longest throw: Player throws from goal line of football field. Distance is measured to where disc lands. Distance is measured in a straight line on the field. Each cone represents 20 yards.

Air time: When ready, the competitor throws the disc. Time is started on release, and stopped when the disc lands on the ground.

Field goals: Competitor attempts to throw a Frisbee through the uprights. Cones will be laid out in 10-yard increments. Each competitor gets three throws. A successful throw receives a score equal to the distance (30 yards = 30 points).

Frisbee archery: Three large circles will be laid out on the ground in the form of a bulls-eye. The smallest center circle is worth 30 points, second circle worth 15, and largest circle worth 5 points. Each competitor gets three throws. Points are awarded only if entire disc is inside the circle (does not count if any part of the disc is touching the rope).

Carnival Frisbee: A stack of 10 cups set on each other in the shape of a pyramid. Competitor stands at a distance of 15 feet (marked by a cone). Throws Frisbee at pyramid. Each cup that falls is worth 1 point. After first throw, competitor sets cups back up and throws again. Again the number of cups knocked down is counted. Repeat one more time.

Scoring the Results

First place in the event: 10 points

Second place in the event: 5 points

Third place in the event: 3 points

- Points contribute to the teams' overall season points.
- Winner of Frisbee Olympics receives an additional 15 points

Figure 10.2   Sample skill challenge series as a culminating event.

Adapted from Chris Bortnem 2000.

1. Championship games. Depending on how the seasonal competition is organized, this may involve several games with small-sided teams from each of the larger class teams who have competed in divisions that are typically for different skill levels.

2. Awards day. Often special guests are invited to present awards (e.g., team awards, fair play, refereeing, coaching). The guests may be school principals, community members, or sport figures. Often local press representatives are invited to garner publicity for the program and the students. From a program advocacy perspective, the importance of having regular local press exposure should not be underestimated. In days of continuing time allotment and budget concerns, a public that is better informed of the quality of the physical education program will be more likely to support the program.

3. Great game day. Students enjoy drinks and snacks as they watch a videotape of a classic game of the sport that has been the focus of their season.

Super Bowl Day at Ogeltree Middle School

9:30 a.m. Tailgate party

Students, teachers, and parents have refreshments prior to the championship game. Students throw and catch footballs on the grass surrounding the tailgate tent.

10:00 a.m. Game time preview

The field is marked with chalk. Student referees are in uniform and ready. A broadcasting table is set up with loudspeakers and students as play by play and commentator broadcasters. Spectators are on the sidelines with teams in either end zone.

10:05 a.m. Introductions

Teams run through banners prepared by students for the occasion. The public address announcer introduces the players from each team. A photographer is taking pictures of all introductions. Cheerleaders (boys and girls) for each team are doing pyramids on the sidelines. The national anthem is played.

10:10 a.m. Game begins

The two teams that made it through the season competition to earn the right to play in the Super Bowl each have one boy and three girls. Referees have been chosen for good performance throughout the season. Both team quarterbacks are girls. Play is lively with especially good defensive play.

At half-time cheerleaders for each team have time to do a prepared set of gymnastics related cheers.

Second-half play is equally good. Game ends in a tie. A brief overtime period is played which also ends in a tie. Teams are named cochampions.

Team and individual awards are presented for players and referees.

Students return to class at 11:00 a.m.

Figure 10.3   A school culminating event in touch football.

4. Video highlights day. Students have taken videos throughout the season as part of a media integration project. They edit the videos and present them to the class as part of the awards day. Students can later check out copies of the video to take home and share with their families. A variation of this idea is to have the championship games of the season videotaped and show them on the awards day.

5. Visit a local sporting venue. A field trip to a local sporting venue for the sport competing by the class during the season can be used to show students how and where the sport is played locally. Representatives from the sport organization might describe to students how they can get involved in the community. Awards might be presented at the community venue rather than at school.

6. Student–staff or student–parent game. Students might compete against teachers or parents in the small-sided games they have played during their season. Awards can be made part of this kind of event also.

7. Between-class competitions. As a culminating event, teams from various classes (e.g., the two sixth grade classes in the school or the three high school classes that have all done similar Sport Education seasons) can compete against each other in an intra-class format.

Culminating events can be videotaped and used for several purposes. The first Sport Education season that was ever taught was done in a Hilliard, Ohio elementary school by physical education teacher Chris Bell. Chris had taken a Sport Education summer workshop from Daryl Siedentop at Ohio State University in 1982. The final requirement of the workshop was to create a Sport Education season plan. The workshop was a mix of full-time doctoral students and part-time Master's students, most of whom were teaching physical education in local schools. Chris created an imaginative gymnastics season plan (Bell, 1994). Teams competed in two levels of compulsory floor exercise as the first competition, then in apparatus work for the second competition of the season. The final performances in each competition were videotaped, primarily to allow Chris to better evaluate her students for report cards. Some of the students asked if they might borrow the videotape to share with their families. When Chris began to get calls and notes from parents saying how excited their sons and daughters were and how much they enjoyed watching the videotape together as a family, we began to understand the power of making things special for kids and sharing these special moments outside the class. The quality of the performances of these fifth and sixth graders and the degree to which they were able to perform as teams in a gymnastics competition astounded the parents and they became immediately supportive of the physical education program. The lesson here is straightforward: What became important to the children became important to their parents. Creating a festive atmosphere for learning and competing helps to make the experience important for students.

Festivity is a primary characteristic of Sport Education. Let's face it: For too many students in too many places physical education is a bore. It is especially true for students in their transitional adolescent years. Creating a festive atmosphere for Sport Education is a reasonably low-cost endeavor. Bulletin boards, awards, special recognition times, and the like do not have to be expensive in terms of cash outlays or teacher time. Students can and should be enlisted to help in creating these elements of festivity. A major potential payoff here is that students get excited about their physical education experience and put more of their own effort into the season. If they then share that excitement with their parents, the physical education program and teacher are likely to get much more support.

Chapter 11

Integrating Academic Goals With Sport Education and Extending Participation

When students leave school each day, the world they enter does not exist in single chunks called subjects, and the activities in which they take part and the problems they face do not come in 30- or 40-minute time spans defined by school subjects. In other words, the worlds of sport, fitness, and leisure are not organized quite like school subjects. The way that schools typically fragment knowledge and skills into subjects, imparted through a curriculum, is not always a good representation of the way things work in the world outside of school.

In addressing this particular topic, many educators have suggested that schools need to implement integrated or interdisciplinary curricula. Integrating school subjects in ways that emphasize their connection to the larger world is one way of helping students see the value of schools and learning and be better able to apply the learning outside of school. Regardless of whether a school curriculum is organized into traditional subjects or integrated in some manner, Sport Education has abundant opportunity to treat the content of a season in ways that integrate nicely with what students are studying in the other parts of the school curriculum.

To understand the possibilities for Sport Education, you need to understand two important terms: interdisciplinary curricula and integrated curricula (Placek, 2003). An interdisciplinary curriculum uses activities in the subject being taught as a way of reinforcing knowledge and skill in other curricular areas. For example, during a third grade physical education lesson, a teacher might introduce a game called math tag. In this game, two or three student chasers try to tag as many of the other students as possible. Upon being tagged, children freeze, raise their hand, and say, "I need a math problem." A student approaches and gives each frozen student a math problem. The frozen student must answer the problem correctly before he or she is unfrozen. Only one person can give a frozen child a math problem, and the person who is giving the problem is not eligible to be tagged. Another example of interdisciplinary teaching would occur when students in a language arts classroom are asked to write an essay on the importance of physical fitness and healthful lifestyles. In an interdisciplinary curriculum, teachers try to cross-fertilize knowledge and skills among subjects.

An integrated curriculum, on the other hand, has much less clear subject boundaries and is usually organized around themes, or at an even more complex level,

Chapter Slides

Links to the World

called big ideas (Beane, 1997). These big ideas may be significant topics about personal development or social topics such as pollution, technology, or international conflict. Themes are not the same as traditional school subjects. They can, however, be explored in conjunction with those subjects. For example, the theme of justice and equity might be pursued by social studies, English, science, and physical education teachers at a middle school level. A social studies teacher would explore changes in justice and equity issues, while an English teacher would explore literature with the main theme of justice and equity. A science teacher might review innovations in science over the past fifty years and how they have impacted justice and equity in society. A physical educator would look at issues of justice and equity in school sport, community sport, and professional sport. In an integrated curriculum, these teachers would not be acting independently but would work as a team so that each teacher's planning would be done with the knowledge of what the others were doing.

Sport Education and Language Arts

Sport Education can be used to foster interdisciplinary efforts in several ways. The first way is by using elements of the Sport Education season to infuse into content in other subjects, such as math, science, **language arts,** or social studies. For example, in a track and field or aerobics season, a science teacher might use what the students are experiencing to teach concepts about the cardiovascular system and how strength is developed and maintained. The second way is by incorporating knowledge and concepts from other subjects into a Sport Education season. For example, if students are studying about Europe in their social studies class, teams for a season could represent **European countries,** with students required to learn about the nation's flag, anthem, geography, and political system. Another example is for students to read about the particular sport as it is portrayed in history, poetry, biographies, or novels. Finally, Sport Education might become part of an integrated curriculum developed around themes.

Links to the World

This chapter will show how Sport Education material can be used in classroom subjects, how grade-level academic goals in subjects such as mathematics, science, literacy, art, and music, among others, can be integrated in a Sport Education season, and how a thematic approach can easily accommodate and be enhanced through the Sport Education model (e.g., using the concept of Olympism across all subject areas).

Chapter Slides

USING SPORT EDUCATION RESOURCES TO ENHANCE CLASSROOM LEARNING

Students generate a significant amount of material during a Sport Education season. For example, they generate score sheets, statistics sheets, and match reports, to name a few. As part of the affiliation of students through the use of persisting teams, students will often design team posters or create representations of a chosen team mascot. All of these areas of Sport Education can be taken by the classroom teachers and used within their subject areas. Some specific examples are discussed next.

Taking Competition Scores for Use in Mathematics Lessons

During any one Sport Education lesson, many numbers are generated. These numbers can include game scores, match statistics, times kept, or the amount of weight lifted. A creative classroom teacher could use these materials to frame any number of mathematical problems. For example:

- *Percentages*. "What percent of your team's total score came from free throws in today's basketball lesson?" "What percent of the total possible score did the Lions team shoot in their archery practice today, and what percent of that score did each team member contribute?"

- *Fractions*. "Express as a fraction, the weight you lifted on the bench press today compared to the weight you lifted on the leg press." "John scored one third of his team's points, and Jennifer scored two fifths. What was their total contribution?"

- *Graphs*. "Draw a line graph of your time for today's mile run, using each of the four laps as the horizontal axis labels." "Look at the graph for the Eagles' football scores for the past week. Which day did they have their best defensive effort?"

- *Calculus*. "Calculate the equation that best fits the Devils' scoring trends from touchdowns and field goals."

Writing Game and Match Reports and Journal Articles in Language Classes

One of the strong growth industries in sport has been the increase in sport journalism. Newspapers now no longer simply report scores and game highlights, but offer detailed explanations of sporting events. Given that team practices and competition in Sport Education are so authentic, language arts teachers have a ready supply of material that students may use. For example:

- *Game and match reports*. "Using the format found in most major newspapers (e.g., headlines, by-lines, story), write a report on the game your team participated in today (as either contestant or official)." "Prepare a press release headline of the major outcome of your Sport Education lesson today."

- *Essays*. "It has been suggested to me that team harmony is important to team success. Write a one-page essay describing the level of team harmony on your Sport Education team this season."

- *Letter writing*. "Write a letter to a potential sponsor for your orienteering team. Include the correct address format, the appropriate formatting, and the acceptable ways of addressing the reader (depending on whether or not he or she is known to you). Try to convince the potential sponsor of the value of providing resources to sponsor a team."

- *Public speaking*. "Next Tuesday, you are to conduct an oral interview with the referee from one of that day's floor hockey matches. Prepare your list of questions, and be prepared to include any specific incidents you might witness during the match on that day."

Using Sport Education Data and Experiences in Science Classes

Science teachers may use data collected in Sport Education to enhance explanations and understanding of science content. A number of sports exist in which human physiology is significantly related to athletic success. Indeed, studying science concepts through their applications to sport may be the most effective way of presenting the content matter. For example:

• *Anatomy and physiology.* The link between human anatomy and physiology as studied in science classes and physical education is clear-cut. It would not be difficult for students to record their heart rates during and after exercise over multiple days and estimate their aerobic capacity as a science project. In a Sport Education fitness season, this connection would be even stronger. Science teachers could use a strength training season to teach both the anatomy of the body and the muscles that move the bony structure at joints. Focus would be on the lifts themselves with identification of which muscles were involved in each type of lift or in using particular machines. Teachers and students could explore how the body adapts to strength training in terms of muscle changes, flexibility, and the impact of strength training on metabolism.

• *Health-related physical activity.* Students could plot steps a day recorded on pedometers or chart their repetitions and weight lifted in a series of strength exercises. One elementary physical education teacher in Columbus, Ohio worked with classroom teachers to have students plot all their walking over the course of a school year. The goal for students was to choose another city named Columbus in a different state and see if they could walk to that Columbus during the school year. A walking trail was created at the school and classroom teachers had their students measure the distance from school to their homes so that when they walked to school they could count the miles they accumulated.

• *Levers and mechanical systems.* During a gymnastics season, teachers could ask teams to analyze the key mechanical systems involved in a balance, roll, or somersault. In weight training seasons, the effect of levers are particularly relevant, because some lifts are performed standing while others are performed from a prone position. The differences in mechanics of lifts would be investigated.

14
Chapter Slides

APPLYING CLASSROOM STUDIES TO THE SPORT EDUCATION SEASON

As materials from Sport Education can be used to enhance classroom learning, an equally large number of opportunities exist in which Sport Education seasons can be used to complement classroom work and help reinforce that knowledge, particularly where the classroom work has a direct application.

An example of an interdisciplinary approach involves students participating in a season of soccer. Their class at the time is studying Europe in social studies. As a result, each of the teams in this Sport Education soccer season take an affiliation with one of the European countries. The soccer team names are taken from a premier team in their adopted country. Students are required to not only take the name of this team, but the team colors, mascot, and the city they represent within that country. In social studies, students learn about these countries. As a special project, the team writes to the chambers of commerce of these cities (or students search the Internet) to get details about the history, geography, and economics of the city and country.

Another example involves social studies students focusing on reading and drawing maps, with a particular emphasis on the concept of scale. In this example, the concurrent Sport Education season is a cross country walking and running season. Using a topographic map of the school grounds, the students plan various courses for use during each Fridays' cross country team competition. Each week a different team will act as the host team and plan the route.

The students not only design the course using the school map, but also determine the distance of the course using the scale on the map. The students check the accuracy of their scale drawing by physically checking the length of the course with a measuring wheel. The organizing team hands out maps of the course two days before competition, so that all teams can walk or run the course to become familiar with the geography and determine their strategy.

INTERDISCIPLINARY SEASON PLANS

14
Chapter Slides

It is possible to plan entire Sport Education seasons in which exist substantial interdisciplinary connections to social studies, art, music, mathematics, science, and literature. This interdisciplinary approach is about making connections—connections that make learning meaningful for students and teachers in these subject areas. The physical education teacher could contribute to and reinforce content that is being taught in these other areas. Likewise, teachers in social studies and math could also work to reinforce content being taught in physical education; that is, they could be working to strengthen the interdisciplinary nature of the curriculum also, although we will not focus on the classroom teacher possibilities here. If classroom teachers and physical education teachers work together so as to mutually support learning in each of the areas, the lines between interdisciplinary and integrated get blurred considerably. The plans we show here assume that the curriculum is still organized around traditional subjects (PE, social studies, math, and the like) but that teachers cooperate to integrate certain aspects of their subjects.

Three sample seasons are presented in this chapter. Each of these examples involves a significant amount of collaboration between the physical education and classroom teachers. This collaboration functions to produce an educational experience in which the various classes students attend during the course of the season will be interconnected to reinforce learning in each separate subject.

Stomp

This season sees a contribution by teachers in physical education, music, and social studies to bring to life the struggles of oppressed minority groups, and their efforts to express themselves through unique music and movement.

Theme

To replicate the percussion-based dance form, called Stomp, that is popular in major cities in which significant Caribbean immigrant populations exist.

Subject Area Contributions

- Music
  - Develop instruments from ordinary household utensils.
  - Learn percussion skills using these instruments.
  - Learn differences in cadence, accent, and beat.
- Sport Education
  - Learn step forms.
  - Design and practice sequences and routines.
- Social studies
  - Examine the role of expressive movement and dance in minority cultures, particularly those who have been oppressed.

- Learn the countries from which immigrants come and the countries to which they immigrate and what their living conditions are.

General Procedures

- Students are in teams of four to six, depending on class size.
- Each week a team is allowed to add one new instrument of accompaniment, but the first one is just the sounds they can make with their feet.
- Teams can choose whatever they wish to use, but it must be a basic household item (e.g., a trash can lid, broom, pan).
- Friday is performance day. Teams present versions of their continuously building routine.
- The other days of the week are used for skill development and routine design.
- On competition Friday one representative from each team acts on a judging panel. The judging panel awards points based on choreography, technique, and coordination among group members.
- Weekly points are accumulated of progressively more points. The final production counts for the largest number of points toward the seasonal championship.
- The season culminates with a final performance that includes costumes and to which other classes are invited.

NASCAR

In this example, students build small cars and race them. This season provides an integrated curriculum within science, math, social studies, and physical education that is strongly grounded in situated learning and cognition. The key to this entire season is that it revolves around content-based accountability; that is, if students make errors in math with regard to their fuel calculations or in science with regard to their mechanics, their cars stop! This example would be particularly interesting for the upper middle school grades.

Theme

Students participate in a season of NASCAR in which they build their own machines, and race on replicated F1 tracks. Other subject integrations are also possible.

Subject Area Contributions and Responsibilities

- Science
  - Students build their race cars. They have a centrifugal clutch, so the car has to be pushed to reach a certain velocity before the fuel motor will kick in. The design of the cars presents opportunities for the students but the size has to be relatively small because of the limit of the 3HP motor (see following text).
  - Motors are 3HP lawn mower engines obtained from a local engine supplier.
  - Learn about mechanics, streamlining, fuels, power, weight distributions, and so on.
- Math
  - All algebra and calculus problems revolve around fuel consumption. (Students get a limited fuel supply each week.)
  - Race courses change weekly, and involve taking the plans from

worldwide F1 courses and working on ratios and proportions to create a scale course on the school grounds.

- Social studies
  - Students write to local industries for sponsorships for their cars.
  - They examine the role of racing in southern communities in the United States.
  - Students could do research on the economic impact of NASCAR racing.

Sport Education

- Races take place during physical education class time.
- Because cars must be propelled to reach a certain speed, students have to train to get fit and strong enough to start the cars. (Starting quickly and as a team gains a competitive advantage.)
- If a car runs out of gas or stalls during racing, the whole team has to run to the point of breakdown and restart the engine.

General Procedures

- Students are in teams of five or six.
- Each Friday is race day, with a different course driven each week.
- Races are time trials (for safety) with teams completing a designated number of laps.
  - A different student must be the driver each week.
  - Each team must have one stop-and-go pit stop during its time trial.
  - Points are awarded weekly and accumulate as a league system would in racing.
- Each week, one team is designated as the circuit team. Their responsibilities are as follows:
  - Take the F1 plan and re-create it with marker cones on the school grounds designated for this event.
  - Act as race officials, with timing, pit judges, and course judges being the major roles. (Officials also invoke time penalties for teams that run off course.)
  - Collate results and provide press coverage of the race.
- During non-race days, teams will practice physical skills of starting and driving and do time trials with their cars. Recall however, that fuel is limited, and more significantly, students of different weights will have impact on the fuel consumptions. Planning is necessary, particularly in math class.
- Racing teams on Fridays will provide one driver and a pit crew. The pit crew will
  - be responsible for starting the car at the beginning of the time trial, and restarting the car in cases of breakdown or stalling,
  - perform the stop-and-go section in pit row, where the car must come to rest and then resume racing, and
  - be responsible for getting the car over the finish line if it runs out of gas or has some other mishap.

World League

This season provides an integrated curriculum within social studies, language arts, and physical education. It is designed around the central themes of government and law. During the season, students create new countries, which they the represent throughout the season. Particular focus in social studies and language arts is given to forms of government and methods for governing. Members of each of the new country teams will also create a national game for that country.

Theme

Students design new countries, complete with national sports. In physical education, they teach students from other countries the sport they have designed, and the culminating event is an Olympic-type festival where all countries compete in these new games. Thus, the number of games in the sport festival is determined by the number of teams in this season.

Subject Area Contributions and Responsibilities

- Social studies
  - Students create new countries, focusing on the concept of government and citizenship.
  - National governing systems are designed (e.g., parliaments, senates, representative houses), together with a constitution, a flag, and national emblems.
- Sport Education
  - Each team has to design a national game. Teachers should probably require that teams design various types of games so that the festival is representative of various types of sports (e.g., invasion games, court-divided game, sector game).
  - Students teach members of other teams the game they have created to represent their nation.
  - Students compete in round-robin tournaments for each of the new games.
- Language arts
  - Students create written descriptions of government protocols and documents, such as voting rights, the electoral process, and the provision of government services.
  - Students create statements of creeds, and a justification of why the particular form of government (e.g., republic, social democracy, single leader) has been chosen.
- Art
  - Students create a concept for the flag and then produce a flag.
  - Students design and create a national mural or emblem.

General Procedures

- Students are in teams of six.
- Games are created and taught to other teams.
- Teams practice each newly taught game including rules, scoring, and officiating.
- Small-sided round-robin tournaments are planned for each game.
- The culminating event is an Olympic-type festival with flags, emblems, and competitions in each game form. These competitions are small-sided so that teams must choose who from their team will represent their country in that competition. All students must have equal playing opportunity in the festival.

*I*n health education, the outcome strands of human development and relationships worked in well with the team aspects of Sport Education. In art they were designing posters, covers for their journals, and team sheets. In technology, on the computer, they were doing word-processing linking to language and much of the publicity generated in this way including writing information for the newsletter.

—Classroom teacher, Australia

AN INTEGRATED CURRICULUM: THE OLYMPIC CURRICULUM

14
Chapter Slides

10
Olympics

As mentioned previously, a truly integrated curriculum is usually organized around themes or big ideas rather than traditional subjects. Most students and teachers are very aware of the **Olympic Games,** which are perhaps the greatest sport festivals in history. Few are aware, however, of the educational movement called Olympism, the term used by Baron Pierre de Coubertin, the founder of the modern Olympic Games, to describe the plan of educational reform he hoped would be sparked by the rejuvenation of the Olympic Games in 1896. From the outside, the concept of Olympism was an educational philosophy that sought to integrate academic study, aesthetic education, moral education, and physical education (Lucas, 1981). The catalyst for this integration was sport; thus the Sport Education model is an appropriate vehicle through which to articulate modern physical education.

Olympism itself is founded in the principles of the Olympic Charter, which describes the purpose of the Olympic movement to "educate young people through sport in a spirit of better understanding between each other and of friendship, thereby helping to build a better and more peaceful world" (USOC Educational Committee, p. 13). However, this concept extends beyond sport. A significant wording of the Olympic creed lies in the following: "The most significant part (in the Olympic Games) is not to win, but to take part. Just as the most important thing in life is not the triumph but the struggle. The essential thing is not to have conquered but to have fought well" (p. 17). Designing an integrated curriculum around the concept (or big idea) of Olympism, then, focuses on the principles of taking part, overcoming obstacles, and striving to be the best you can be.

The effort described here—to develop a curriculum integrated around the theme of Olympism—works best if it is pursued for a semester or a full school year. What follows is a standard format that could be adapted to meet the constraints of local curricular schedules.

• *Organizing the school year.* The school year should be divided into four or five seasons, each lasting seven to nine weeks. Season length is necessary to accomplish the diverse goals of the Olympic curriculum.

• *The national team as the affiliation format.* Teams represent nations (preferably spread across the several continents). **Nations** can be chosen by teams or assigned by teachers. Teams remain intact for that season, then new nations are chosen and teams can be reorganized to provide even competition or for other reasons.

11
Links to the World

• *The Olympic committee.* Many teachers have chosen to include a sport committee or sports board as an element of added student responsibility in Sport

Education. This feature is particularly beneficial in middle and secondary school because it provides a major role for students and creates a mechanism whereby decisions can be made and disputes arbitrated by students themselves, thus contributing to the personal growth goals of the curriculum. The sports board would, when grounded in Olympism, function as an Olympic Committee.

• *Choosing the sports.* Any season should focus on a different Olympic sport. Selection of sports is left to the individual teachers, schools, or districts. Sports should be selected that represent different combinations of strength, skill, strategy, and aesthetic qualities. As in all Sport Education seasons, small-sided, modified sports are preferred, allowing for progressive skill and strategy development as well as more active participation by all students.

Links to the World

National Anthems

• *Integrating academic work to meet the global, multicultural, and aesthetic education goals.* During the season in which students represent a national team, they learn about the **country** they represent as well as those represented by classmates. The accompanying CD-ROM includes information to help teachers direct teams to research background information about the country they represent, as well as a sample table of contents of a report documenting their assigned country. The feature allows for substantial integration with social studies, art, music, and literature. National colors and **anthems** can be used to add to the festive atmosphere. Music, art, and poetry from the various nations can be incorporated as appropriate. Much of this research can be done as homework or integrated with the classroom teacher's work. Students can also learn about the national sports of each country and their major sport figures. Students might create their own Olympic awards as art projects.

Fair Play Resources

• *Formalizing the personal development goals of the curriculum.* Olympism is dedicated to creating a more peaceful world, working together, friendly competition, and learning to strive to be the best that you can be. The personal and social development goals of Olympism are central to its overall purposes. Chapter 7 explains in detail the **fair play** approach to behavior and social development that is consistent with the goals of Sport Education. The examples of fair play systems described in that chapter can easily be adapted to an Olympic fair play system. This system could also include player and referee oaths that are given formally by a representative at the start of each competition.

Olympics

• *Creating a festive Olympic atmosphere.* The Olympic movement provides many symbols, rituals, and ceremonies that can be easily incorporated into the Olympic curriculum to develop and sustain a festive atmosphere. Suggestions include using the **Olympic** rings and creed as large, permanent posters in the gym, using the athlete and referee oaths prior to the beginning of each season's competition, and playing the **Olympic** hymn during the seasonal award ceremonies. Teachers can also use materials from the countries represented by national teams to build and sustain a festive atmosphere. Suggestions include using national flags and national colors, having students develop bulletin boards providing information and pictures of their home countries, and using national anthems in medal ceremonies.

This standard format could be adapted to local needs, yet still maintain the underlying structural principles. Some schools might want to have more slightly shorter seasons. Some schools might want to keep students on teams for an entire semester or school year. Some teachers might want to emphasize personal growth in the curriculum and downplay the aesthetics or global education. Some teachers will find it difficult to integrate art, music, and literature as fully as they desire. None of these restrictions or differences in outlook need detract from pursuing the main goals of the Olympic curriculum.

It is also advisable for teachers to begin the Olympic curriculum effort with a basic model, implement it well, and then add to it as students become accustomed to the model and teachers have more time to devote to generating resources for developing the model more fully. For example, when students have projects to develop information about the nation they represent, the materials from these projects can be used in later years, thus building a backlog of Olympic curriculum resources. Also, as teachers in the school learn about the Olympic curriculum, they will see ways they can contribute to it through student work and projects in various classes, especially in art, music, and literature, but also in social studies.

> **U**nder Sport Education, student-centered teaching offers new responsibilities to learners and the real possibility of cross-curriculum teaching to classroom teachers. The pedagogy is compatible with classroom teachers' propositions about teaching and may become one basis for a new, professional developing relationship between specialists and the classroom teacher.
>
> —Taggart, Medland, & Alexander, 1995 p. 18

EXTENDING PARTICIPATION OUTSIDE OF CLASS

Chapter Slides

A goal of Sport Education is for students to decide voluntarily to participate in sport, fitness, and recreational activities outside of class. This goal is fully consistent with the current focus in physical education to help students develop physically active lifestyles (Siedentop, 2004). For students to move toward a lifestyle commitment to physical activity, they must come to value activity so much that they are willing to make choices for participation in light of other attractive, competing choices for how to spend their time. Sport Education is a particularly good curriculum and instruction model through which to achieve that goal because it tends to empower students and fully engage them in the learning and management of their own sport experiences.

Students come to value things that they enjoy, they are able to do fairly well, they have knowledge of, have a social element, and they have become invested in. Evaluations of Sport Education tend to support the contention that many students do enjoy it, get better at the activity and feel comfortable performing, enjoy the camaraderie of team affiliation, and become quite invested in helping to make the team and season work well for all. Thus, it is fair to say that Sport Education has a good chance to influence lifestyle choices.

Recall, however, that our goal here is to get students involved in activity outside of their class time and outside of school. These two subgoals are different, so we will address them individually.

Extending School-Based Participation Outside of Class Time

Sport Education teachers have found many ways to extend participation outside of regularly scheduled physical education class time, and students in many settings have been observed to be practicing their skills outside of class time. Among the options available to teachers are the following:

- *Recess practice at the elementary level.* Teams can gain points toward the seasonal championship if they have a practice plan and use the time allotted to recess to have a team practice. In secondary schools, teams can gather during periods of nonattached time and where the needed facility is available. For example, team players can meet during periods of open gym and hold team practices.

- *Intramural involvement.* Middle and high schools that have intramural programs for students can be used to encourage students to sign up to join an intramural team or to have teams from the Sport Education season sign up together as a team.

- *Inter-class competitions.* Nonattached time during the school day can be used to organize inter-class competitions. For example, after an Olympic gymnastics season done by several classes in physical education, inter-class competitions can be organized for beam, floor exercise, vaulting, and other events. In a team sport season, teams that finished at various levels in the seasonal championship can be pitted against one another in inter-class competitions (e.g., 1v1, 2v2, and the like).

- *Festival event.* This event can be planned much as a school assembly would be planned. For example, if aerobic or folk dance were the focus of a Sport Education season, an assembly could be planned to have groups perform their final routines or dances. This example is very much in line with the traditions in international sport competitions such as the Winter Olympics where, following the completion of formal competition in figure skating, the skaters hold a skating exhibition.

Logging Out-of-School Physical Activity

Student engagement in **out-of-class team practices** and intramural competitions is a gauge of the physical education program's contribution to students being physically active beyond the program. Periodic assessment of such engagement can offer important information in terms of the program's impact. The accompanying CD-ROM offers some examples of assessment tools that can be used for that purpose.

Extending Participation Outside of School Time

If students are to participate outside of school, they must learn more about where and how to participate and be encouraged to become involved in opportunities outside of the school physical education, intramural, or interscholastic sport programs. This is especially important because lifestyle commitment must eventually be played out in a community or private setting. Students can be educated and encouraged in many ways, some of which are discussed here:

- *Finding out where a sport is played in the community.* Students and teams can be given homework assignments that focus on learning about how a sport that is the focus for a particular Sport Education season is organized in a community. For example, in a Sport Education volleyball season, assignments might be to find out where volleyball is offered either as a drop-in activity or in league play, what age groups participate, how much it costs, when participation opportunities are offered, and who typically participates (age, gender, ethnicity, and so on). Each team may be given a portion of this assignment and have to report to the class. Alternatively, the class could produce a guidebook for volleyball in the community.

- *Participation homework.* In some school settings, where students likely live in the same neighborhoods, homework that is participation-oriented can be assigned. It can range from skill practice to team workouts.

- *Field trip day.* At the end of a Sport Education season, it can be useful to take classes to a local venue where a particular sport is offered. For example, at the end of one tennis season in a New Zealand high school, teams visited the local private tennis club. They were given information about membership and opportunities and they were allowed to experience playing tennis in a club facility.

- *Internet searches.* While the community discovery project previously described focuses exclusively on opportunities in the local area, another valuable exercise is to have students search the Internet to learn more about the sport or activity. Questions to research include: What are the major national organizations? Do they sponsor age-group involvement? Do sport-specific clubs exist in your region? Do opportunities exist to learn more about tactics and skills for this sport on the Internet? How does one get involved as a coach? Do coaching credentials exist to be earned? How does one get involved as an official? Do officiating credentials exist to be earned?

- *Linking with local private sport clubs and organizations.* Teachers could contact local clubs and arrange for students to use club facilities for a period of time (or pay a reduced fee, if necessary) following the completion of a Sport Education season. This strategy would be particularly useful for activities such as golf and bowling where several local opportunities are likely to exist.

- *Linking with local sport stores.* Teachers could explore arrangements with local sport outfitters for students to get reduced rates on renting equipment. For example, following Sport Education seasons such as in-line skating, roller hockey, climbing, hiking, and other outdoor pursuit activities, local stores could provide reduced rental charges for a specified time. Students could experience activities such as cross-country skiing, snowshoeing, rock climbing, and in-line skating. Both the physical education program and the local business would benefit, because students would learn more about activities in the community and outfitters would make contact with potential customers.

Time is the most precious commodity in schools. No teacher of any subject feels that he or she has sufficient time to do all they want to do. Certainly, in physical education classes, teachers do not have sufficient time to reach significant goals in many areas. Sport Education uses longer units (seasons) to allow sufficient time for students to make meaningful progress in a particular activity. This chapter has shown ways in which students can be motivated to use out-of-class time (nonattached school time and out-of-school time) to participate in an activity and to learn more about how they can get involved with that activity in other venues in the community. In addition, the chapter showed how learning in various subject areas can be strengthened through integrated and interdisciplinary planning and teaching.

References

Alexander, K., Taggart, A., & Luckman, J. (1998). Pilgrims progress: The sport education crusade down under. *Journal of Physical Education, Recreation and Dance, 69*(4), 21-23.

Almond, L. (1986). Primary and secondary rules in games. In R. Thorpe et al., *Rethinking games teaching* (pp. 73-74). Loughborough, England: University of Technology, Dept. of Physical Education and Sports Science.

Beane, J. (1997). *Curriculum integration.* New York: Teachers College Press.

Bell, C. (1994). Elementary gymnastics. In D. Siedentop, (ed.), *Sport education: Quality PE through positive sport experiences* (pp. 47-60). Champaign, IL: Human Kinetics.

Bell, C., & Darnell, J. (1994). Elementary soccer. In D. Siedentop, (ed.), *Sport education: Quality PE through positive sport experiences* (pp. 37-46). Champaign, IL: Human Kinetics.

Bortnam, C. (2000). Ultimate Frisbee high school work sample. Unpublished document, Corvallis, Oregon: Oregon State University.

Carlson, T. (1995a). "Now I think I can." The reaction of eight low-skilled students to sport education. *ACHPER Healthy Lifestyles Journal, 42*(4), 6-8.

Carlson, T.B. (1995b). We hate gym: Student alienation from physical education. *Journal of Teaching in Physical Education, 14,* 467-477.

Carlson, T.B., & Hastie, P.A. (1997). The student-social system within sport education. *Journal of Teaching in Physical Education, 16,* 176-195.

Coakley, J.J. (1994). *Sport in society: Issues and controversies.* 5th ed. St. Louis: Mosby Year Book.

Cohen, E.G. (1994). *Designing groupwork: Strategies for the heterogeneous classroom.* New York: Teachers College, Columbia University.

Darnell, J. (1994). Sport education in the elementary curriculum. In D. Siedentop, (ed.), *Sport education: Quality PE through positive sport experiences* (pp. 61-71). Champaign, IL: Human Kinetics.

Doyle, W. (1986). Classroom organization and management. In M.C. Wittrock (ed.). *Handbook of research on teaching.* 3rd ed. (pp. 392-431). New York: Macmillan.

Dugas, D. (1994). Sport education in the secondary curriculum. In D. Siedentop, (ed.), *Sport education: Quality PE through positive sport experiences* (pp. 105-112). Champaign, IL: Human Kinetics.

Duquin, M.E. (1988). Gender and youth sport: Reflections on old and new fictions. In F.L. Smoll, (ed.) et al., *Children in sport.* 3rd ed. (pp. 31-41). Champaign, IL: Human Kinetics.

Grant, B.C. (1992). Integrating sport into the physical education curriculum in New Zealand secondary schools. *Quest, 44,* 304-316.

Grant, B.C., Sharp, P., & Siedentop, D. (1992). *Sport education in physical education: A teacher's guide.* Wellington, NZ: Hillary Commission.

Graves, M.A., & Townsend, S. (2000). Applying the sport education curriculum model to dance. *Journal of Physical Education, Recreation and Dance, 71*(8), 50-54.

Gréhaigne, J.F., Godbout, P., Bouthier, D. (1999). The foundations of tactics and strategy in team sports. *Journal of Teaching in Physical Education, 18,* 159-174.

Griffin, P., & Placek, J. (1983). *Fair play in the gym: Race and sex equity in physical education* (pp. 132-133). Amherst, MA: University of Massachusetts, Women's Equity Program.

Hastie, P.A. (1998). Helping middle school students become good officials. *Teaching Elementary Physical Education, 9*(4), 20-21.

Hastie, P.A. (2000). An ecological analysis of a sport education season. *Journal of Teaching in Physical Education, 19*(3), 355-373.

Hellison, D. (1996). Teaching personal and social responsibility in physical education. In S.J. Silverman & C.D. Ennis (eds.), *Student learning in physical education: Applying research to enhance instruction* (pp. 269-286). Champaign, IL: Human Kinetics.

Kinchin, G.D. (2001). Using team portfolios during a sport education season. *Journal of Physical Education, Recreation and Dance,* 72(2), 41-44.

Kirk, D., & Kinchin, G.D. (2003). Situated learning as a theoretical framework for sport education. *European Physical Education Review,* 9(3), 221-235.

Kirk, D., & Macdonald, D. (1998). Situated learning in physical education. *Journal of Teaching in Physical Education,* 17, 376-387.

Kounin, J.S. (1970). *Discipline and group management in schools.* Huntington, New York: R. E. Krieger Pub. Co.

Launder, A.G. (2001). *Play practice: The games approach to teaching and coaching sports.* Champaign, IL: Human Kinetics.

Loy, J.W., & Kenyon, G.S. (1969). *Sport, culture and society: A reader in the sociology of sport.* New York: Macmillan.

Lucas, J. (1981). History of the Olympic ideal. In C.H. Strong & D.J. Ludwig (eds.), *The Olympic ideal: 776 B.C. to the 21st century: Proceedings of the National Olympic Academy IV* (p. 47-59). May 29-June 1, 1980, Bloomington, IN: Indiana University, School of Health, Physical Education and Recreation.

Mohr, D.J., Townsend, J.S., & Bulger, S.M. (2001). A pedagogical approach to sport education season planning. *Journal of Physical Education, Recreation and Dance,* 72(9), 37-46.

Olafson, L. (2002). "I hate physical education." Adolescent girls talk about physical education. *The Physical Educator,* 59, 67-74.

Placek, J.H. (2003). Interdisciplinary curriculum in physical education: Possibilities and problems. In S. Silverman & C. Ennis, (eds.), *Student learning in physical education: Applying research to enhance instruction.* 2nd ed. (pp. 287-311). Champaign, IL: Human Kinetics.

Pope, C. (1992). Anyone for Sport Education? A Sport Education curriculum model: An ethnographic investigation to student and teacher response. Paper presented at the AARE/ANARE Conference. Deakin University, Geelong, Victoria, Australia.

Pope, C. (1996). Student experiences of a Sport Education curriculum model. Unpublished Master of Education Dissertation, University of Waikato, NZ.

Quindlen, A. (1992). Feeling fully 40, ex-ballplayer exults in Dream Team's excellence. *Columbus Dispatch,* 12 July.

Richardson, M., & Oslin, J.L. (2003). Creating an authentic dance class using sport education. *Journal of Physical Education, Recreation and Dance,* 74(7), 49-55.

Romar, J.E. (1995). *Case studies of Finnish physical education teachers: Espoused and enacted theories of action.* Abo, Finland: Aba Akademi University Press.

Sharan, S., & Sharan, Y. (1992). *Expanding cooperative learning through group investigation.* New York: Teachers College Press.

Sheed, W. (1995, winter). Why sports matter. *Wilson Quarterly,* 11-25.

Siedentop, D. (1994). *Sport education: Quality PE through positive sport experiences.* Champaign, IL: Human Kinetics.

Siedentop, D. (1996). Physical education and education reform: The case of sport education. In S.J. Silverman & C.D. Ennis (eds.), *Student learning in physical education: Applying research to enhance instruction* (pp. 247-267). Champaign, IL: Human Kinetics.

Siedentop, D. (1998). In search of effective teaching: What we have learned from teachers and students. Paper presented at the National Convention of the American Alliance for Health, Physical Education, Recreation and Dance, Reno, NV, 5-9 April.

Siedentop, D. (2002). Sport education: A retrospective. *Journal of Teaching in Physical Education,* 21, 409-418.

Siedentop, D. (2004). *Introduction to physical education, fitness, and sport.* 5th ed. Boston, MA: McGraw-Hill.

Siedentop, D., & Tannehill, D. (2000). *Developing teaching skills in physical education.* 4th ed. Mountain View, CA: Mayfield.

SPARC (Sport and Physical Activity Research Centre). (1994). *Report for the sport education II project.* Canberra: Australian Sports Commission.

SPARC (Sport and Physical Activity Research Centre). (1995). *Report on the 1994 trial of sport education.* Canberra: Australian Sport Commission.

SEPEP (n.d.). Sport education in physical education project, curriculum materials. Perth, W.A.: Edith Cowan University.

Sweeney, J., Tannehill, D., & Teeters, L. (1992). Team up for fitness. *Strategies,* 5(6), 20-23.

Taggart, A., Brown, T., & Alexander, K. (1995). Three schools' approaches to assessment in sport education. *ACHPER Healthy Lifestyles Journal,* 42(4), 12-15.

Taggart, A., Medland, A., & Alexander, K. (1995). "Goodbye superteacher." Teaching sport education in the primary school. *ACHPER Health Lifestyles Journal,* 42(4), 16-18.

Tousignant, M., & Siedentop, D. (1983). A qualitative analysis of tasks structures in required secondary physical education classes. *Journal of Teaching in Physical Education,* 3, 47-57.

Townsend, J.S., Mohr, D.J., Rairigh, R.M., & Bulger, S.M. (2003). *Assessing student outcomes in sport education. NASPE assessment series.* Reston, VA: National Association of Sport and Physical Education.

United States Olympic Education Committee. (n.d.) *Olympic day in the schools.* Champaign, IL: Human Kinetics.

Wiggins, G. (1987, winter). Creating a thought provoking curriculum. *American Educator,* 10: 17.

Wiggins G. (1993). Assessment: Authenticity, context, and validity. *Phi Delta Kappan,* 75(3), 200-214.

Index

Note: The italicized *f* and *t* following page numbers refer to figures and tables, respectively.

About the Authors

Daryl Siedentop, PED, is a professor emeritus at The Ohio State University. He created the Sport Education model in the 1980s and published his first book on the subject, *Sport Education,* in 1994. He is also the author of several books on physical education, curriculum planning, and sports coaching.

Dr. Siedentop earned the 1984 International Olympic Committee President Prize (Samaranch Award) for work in sport pedagogy. He is a fellow of the American Academy of Kinesiology and Physical Education and has received numerous awards, including the Distinguished Alumni Award from Hope College in 1991; the American Alliance for Physical Education, Recreation and Dance (AAHPERD) Alliance Scholar Award in 1994; the National Association for Sport and Physical Education (NASPE) Curriculum and Instruction Academy Honor Award in 1994; the School of HPER Distinguished Alumni Award from Indiana University in 1996; and the AAHPERD Research Consortium McCloy Award in 1998. In his spare time, Dr. Siedentop enjoys golf, exercise, and reading.

Peter A. Hastie, PhD, professor in the department of health and human performance at Auburn University, has conducted numerous seasons of Sport Education in schools and has published more than 10 papers on the topic. He completed the first series of empirical studies on the Sport Education model and presented a keynote speech on the topic at the 2000 Pre-Olympic Scientific Congress. Dr. Hastie is a member of AAHPERD, American Educational Research Association (AERA), and International Association for Physical Education in Higher Education (AIESEP). He enjoys whitewater rafting, traveling, and overland trekking.

Hans van der Mars, PhD, professor in the department of exercise and sport science at Oregon State University, has been a physical education teacher educator for 20 years. He received an Excellence in Teaching Award from Oregon State University in 2001. He has also received two Outstanding Research Presentation Awards from the Association for Behavior Analysis and has been both coeditor and editorial board member of the *Journal of Teaching in Physical Education* as well as reviewer for numerous other research journals. Dr. van der Mars has published extensively on teaching and teacher education in physical education and made more than 100 presentations on teacher education topics at conferences and professional workshops. He enjoys playing golf, jogging and working out, reading, and listening to music in his spare time.

How to Use the CD-ROM

System Requirements

You can use this CD-ROM on either a Windows-based PC or a Macintosh computer.

Windows

- IBM PC compatible with Pentium processor
- Windows 98/2000/XP/Vista
- Adobe Reader 8.0
- Microsoft Word
- Microsoft Office PowerPoint 2003 or higher
- Microsoft Office Excel
- Microsoft Office Publisher
- 4x CD-ROM drive

Macintosh

- Power Mac recommended
- System 10.4 or higher
- Adobe Reader
- Microsoft Word
- Microsoft Office PowerPoint 2004 for MAC or higher
- Microsoft Office Excel
- Microsoft Office Publisher
- 4x CD-ROM drive

User Instructions

Windows

1. Insert the *Complete Guide to Sport Education* CD-ROM. (Note: The CD-ROM must be present in the drive at all times.)
2. Select the "My Computer" icon from the desktop.
3. Select the CD-ROM drive.
4. Open the file you wish to view. See the "00Start.pdf" file for a list of the contents.

Macintosh

1. Insert the *Complete Guide to Sport Education* CD-ROM. (Note: The CD-ROM must be present in the drive at all times.)
2. Double-click the CD icon located on the desktop.
3. Open the file you wish to view. See the "00Start" file for a list of the contents.

For customer support, contact Technical Support:

Phone: 217-351-5076 Monday through Friday (excluding holidays) between 7:00 a.m. and 7:00 p.m. (CST).

Fax: 217-351-2674

E-mail: support@hkusa.com

You'll find
other outstanding
physical education resources at

www.HumanKinetics.com

In the U.S. call

1-800-747-4457

Australia	.08 8372 0999
Canada	1-800-465-7301
Europe	+44 (0) 113 255 5665
New Zealand	0064 9 448 1207

HUMAN KINETICS
The Information Leader in Physical Activity
P.O. Box 5076 • Champaign, IL 61825-5076 USA